edition 'ʌngewʌndtə

Book Series of the
University of Applied Arts Vienna
Edited by Gerald Bast, Rector

IOA STUDIOS HADID LYNN PRIX SELECTED STUDENT WORKS 2009

Edited by Wolf D. Prix

 Springer Wien New York

CONTENTS

Gerald Bast

"IT IS THE DRIVE TOWARDS ACTION AND SOCIAL CHANGE THROUGH ART, SCIENCE AND CULTURE, THE WILL TO MAKE A DIFFERENCE"

Architecture consists of more than form filled with function. Being one of the most visible exponents of all applied arts, architecture requires social responsibility, energy and resource efficiency as well as a permanent drive for innovation and progress. Architecture is about the beauty and excitement of ideas put into reality.

The way one of the most visible forms of all applied arts is taught at the Angewandte clearly aims at countering the wish for hollow, market-driven aestheticism. To break disciplinary boundaries, and regenerate cities, regions, as well as human minds through new and uncommon approaches to reality. Because architecture not only consumes scarce space, if well conducted, it can fill emptiness with content and meaning, enrich cities and countrysides alike.

Architects and planning bodies need to critically ask whether a building will contribute to a socially as well as environmentally sounder form of living? The same way as the economy and politics must never be ends in themselves, art in general and architecture in particular must aim at catering social and environmental needs, thereby trying to shape the future.

Universities are places where students ought to be sheltered from the destructive influences of market forces. Universities ought to be places where students critically reflect on reality and live up to their highest creative potentials, think of ideas, solutions and designs untouched before. Only if we go beyond what is commonly accepted, beyond what is comfortable and easy to reach, will we be able to impact on reality, make a difference, develop advanced forms of social interaction, thereby "building" the future.

It is the drive towards action and social change through art, science and culture, the will to make a difference, which powerful architectural statements, gathered in this publication exhibit most impressively. Trying to make a difference not only is crucial for all of us, it is also what the University of Applied Arts has been founded on – something we try to live up to every single day.

Gerald Bast
President of the University of Applied Arts Vienna

Wolf D. Prix

"NEW SOLUTIONS MUST BE SOUGHT, WHILE SIMPLE SOLUTIONS ARE NO SOLUTIONS AT ALL"

Architecture is the three-dimensional expression of the culture of a society. According to this definition, society and thus also architecture is becoming ever more complex as a result of growing globalization.

However, it is a paradox that the built environment is becoming ever more important for our society while architects are becoming ever less relevant. Schools of architecture must overcome this paradox. This, however, cannot succeed with simply linear solutions. New solutions must be sought, while simple solutions are no solutions at all. Complex solutions are called for.

Training should thus not seek to cultivate the technically well-trained architect assisting in the fulfillment of his clients' dreams. Rather, it should provide the student a chance to develop strategies that can bring forth complex solutions for the built environment of the future – and this with the full awareness that complex solutions can be new but not necessarily optimal.

The Institute of Architecture at the University of Applied Arts is structured in five strategic departments that are a general reflection of the objectives of the institute. The three design studios Architectural Design 1 (Studio Hadid), Architectural Design 2 (Studio Lynn) and Architectural Design 3 (Studio Prix) that all resemble a lab for developing future architectural concepts are complemented by the Cross-Over Studio where young international architects can elaborate their ideas and concepts.

The studios are backed by another department, History and Theory of Architecture (Liane Lefaivre). Students received support in a project-oriented way while working on conceptual designs from the "Strategy of Technology and Material" unit (structural design with Klaus Bollinger, climate design with Brian Cody and building construction.) The "Strategy of Reality" unit gives the students insights into building realities with courses on architecture and politics, strategy of communication and strategy of real estate, showing how seeming constraints can be used to influence the future of our society.

The international networking of the institute offers students not only the possibility of exchanges with other renowned schools of architecture but also the challenge of engaging in a dialogue on diploma and annual projects with internationally renowned architects. By having international experts on its staff the Institute of Architecture ensures a network with schools of architecture all over the world.

Students who want to know what the future of architecture will look like will have to study at the University of Applied Arts Vienna. If you follow Bloch's concept of utopia the future can be read in the traces of the present. It is thus our goal to leave clearly legible traces.

Wolf D. Prix
Dean, Institute of Architecture

IOA
DIPLOMA
PROJECTS

Eva Diem

THE NEW ANGEWANDTE: RAMPGEWANDTE
PROBING INTO THE LIMITS OF SURFACE THICKNESS

Studio Lynn

This thesis project, a new building for the University of Applied Arts Vienna, explores the possibilities of spatial organization, connectivity and architectural effect through the rhythmic extension, lamination, thickening and dissolving of surfaces. The primary architectural system is a large, spatial ramp that threads through the school to create a continuous series of interaction spaces. These spaces act as catalysts for creativity and communication by creating mixing spaces for interdisciplinary and social exchange while also allowing studio spaces to spill into the more spatially open and highly visible zone of the building.

The architectural possibilities latent in surface thickness are central concerns of this project. Computer-generated surfaces are typically infinitely thin, having a mathematical thickness of "0". To deal with the thickness of surface means to understand real, buildable architectural elements with attributes, such as poché, that are created through techniques like lamination. In this project, surface thickness is delineated with multiple, critical design moments along the ramp. Surfaces are manipulated primarily to determine scale in relation to use, however second and third level influences, such as tension or pressure, are used to disturb the primary nature of the geometries and create new properties and effects. The continuity of the ramp surface should primarily be understood for its ability to effect spatial separation, curate circulation and dramatically interweave the program of an art academy, rather than simply a by-product of the material effect of poured-in-place concrete.

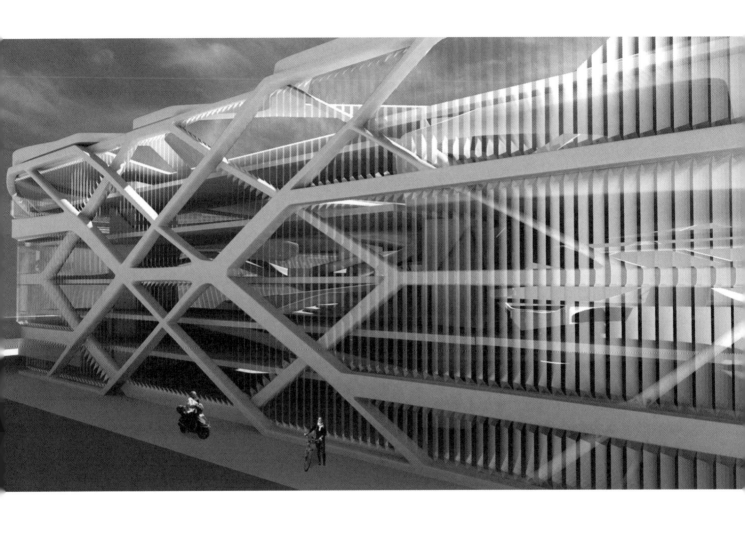

Mihaela Dumitru

ELECTRIC DIE CUT
RETHINKING LONDON'S PRIVATE CLUB

Studio Lynn

The architectural topic of *Electric Die Cut* is the façade, not as an elevation, but as a complex spatial container that deals with mass, carving and geometrical representation. This focus on the façade led to design of a highly visible building that serves as an institution for pop culture, a place where trends are set. What the Beatles were in for 1960s and Studio 54 was for the 1970s, this building imagines for today.

Scenario

The project is a hybrid – part private club and part public concert venue – located in London's south-eastern part, a creative district populated by people who work in art and design. Historically, private clubs in London started as salons – places for the exchange of ideas – for a limited public. Nowadays, a place like this would also need to include a broader public. To accomplish this, the building integrates restaurants, bars and, most importantly, a large concert hall that would be open to everyone. Typical clients of the building would be the so-called "bobos" – urban bourgeois-bohemians who are interested in non-mainstream fashion and culture – and also fans of individual performers. The public program works to increases the prestige, vitality and visibility of the actual private club which still has restricted membership, and is primarily for artists and scensters of the creative arts.

Architecturally I am interested in a deep façade that creates a rich sequence of spatial conditions as it transitions between super-flat exterior surfaces and a richly three-dimensional interior concert hall. Contemporary clubs and venues are typically utilitarian boxes that simply attempt to camouflage the huge machinery needed inside. My proposal takes the box and carves inside to expose a sensuous, jewellery-like interior. The opaque, structural exterior is pushed inside the building through a series of highly-reflective, curvilinear surfaces (nicknamed "trumpets"). As the trumpets push into the building they create a sequence of spaces and habitats that builds one's anticipation and excitement for experiencing the heart of the building.

The private club itself is located at the top of the building. It consists of 15 hotel rooms and an after-hours lounge, located directly above the venue space and just below the hotel rooms and forms a courtyard. The lounge features a water-filled glass surface that mediates between the private club and the venue. Serving as a small swimming pool for the lounge, this trumpet plunges into the venue space below and replaces the traditional disco ball with a lantern that emits filtered, aquatic light. The venue space itself, with its interior façade that creates floor, wall and ceiling, is the clear climax of the building's diverse spatial experiences. This inner façade is generated by the thickening the exterior one. Its general shape is influenced primarily by balconies and the grand staircase that wraps around it but also by the stage requirements: the sound system, lighting equipment and ventilation system. The interior volume accommodates these requirements while also creating its own identity: that of a pregnant, figural surface composed of multiple layers that are materially differentiated, embedded or coincident to it.

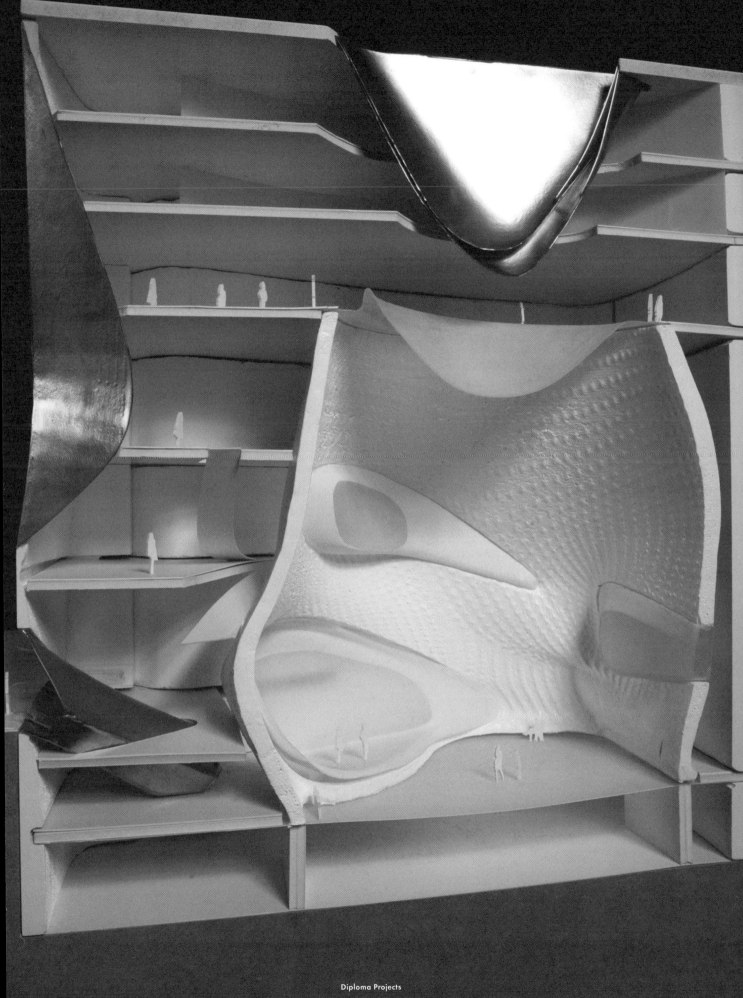

Anna Edthofer

I HEART LA
UP DOWN ATHLETIC CLUB –
UPGRADING DOWNTOWN

Studio Lynn

This project is an extension of the LA Athletic Club in downtown Los Angeles. The extension introduces three new activities to the existing club: climbing, scuba diving and golf. The project focuses on the production of unexpected spatial and atmospheric occurrences through the aggregation and combination of the programmatic zones, each with a unique set of architectural qualities.

Atmospherically, the traditional American athletic club of the 1920s is a rather peculiar place. The architectural program is vertically stacked, producing a distinct and separate world on each level. The resulting building is a series of artificial worlds – replicas based on culturally constructed images of human nature and body culture. As contemporary office work diverges from what the human body was constructed for, there is often a need for the "natural" in the life of the urban worker. The athletic club fulfills this need by mimicking the natural conditions of human activity and locating them in the urban context.

My project diverges from the traditional paradigm of the athletic club by producing hybrid, "super-natural" environments. Rather than insulating activities from one another, the design emphasizes the borders between the zones, articulating them and making them apparent. Hybrid atmospheres and scenarios arise through this complex spatial layering and interweaving. By focusing on the structural and spatial transitions between these atmospherically distinct pieces, my design relates and interlocks the zones into a heterogeneous and spatially, intricate whole.

Julia Futo

ORNAMELT

Studio Lynn

This project is a chocolate factory and flagship store for the Viennese company Niemetz, where visitors can glance into the manufacturing process of the delights. The firm was founded in the late 19th century. Their current coffee shops in Linz and Salzburg, as well as the entire company image, are based on the vibe of the monarchic coffeehouses of fin de siècle Vienna. The project is in the center of the 1st district on a corner site facing a long plaza, Neuer Markt. Other imperial pastry shops such as Demel, Gerstner, Oberlaa and Heiner are also very close. In this project, visitors can follow the different conditions of chocolate, from powder through liquid to solid, while touring the building. Through an orchestrated sequence of public spaces they continuously become closer to the products.

The goal of this project is to develop a formal language drawing on neo-classic ornaments and, in an architectural way, explore the different material conditions of chocolate which spans from liquid to solid, each state having characteristic surface and structural qualities. Just as molded chocolates are simultaneously surface and ornament, this project shows that ornament as frieze, cornice and relief are not only decorative, but have the potential to become structural and volumetric while keeping their qualities like softness and plasticity. The intention is to melt ornamented graphical surface into structural ornament.

The building itself becomes a machine with all technical equipment molded into the floor slabs and walls. These "molded pockets" also work on a larger scale. The public area that pushes through the building as an open volume is a set of large pockets. These split-level pockets allow the visitors to observe the manufacturing process from above or be part of the machinery by seeing it from below. The pockets dissolve from solid surface to structure to create transparency and visually connect the fabrication and display areas.

Structurally, the fiber-cast concrete pockets and inclined interior walls transfer forces to the foundation. They dissolve from solid surface to structure in order to create transparency and also from the inside to the outside, where the façade has a load-bearing function.

The inclined interior walls of the project are consistent with façade diagrid in both angle and position. The structure is expressed as relief on the solid surface, where fabrication areas need controlled light conditions. This surface gradually opens up in the public areas to let natural light in. Merging environmental and ornamental performance, the façade thickens up around the openings to create sun shading. Cool air is led through the atrium into double floor slabs and from here it is distributed. Used hot air is exhausted through the façade.

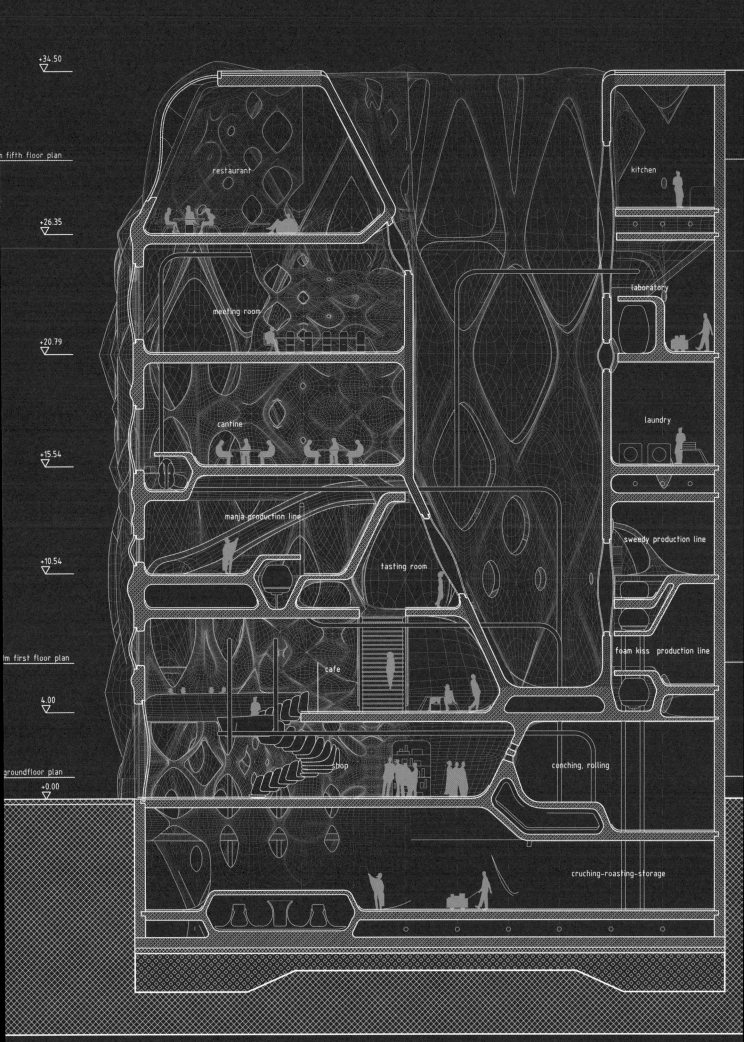

section A-A scale 1:100

+34.50

fifth floor plan

+26.35

+20.79

+15.54

+10.54

first floor plan

4.00

groundfloor plan
+0.00

restaurant

meeting room

cantine

manja production line

tasting room

cafe

shop

kitchen

laboratory

laundry

sweedy production line

foam kiss production line

conching, rolling

cruching-roasting-storage

Lukas Galehr

BAD VIENNA
PERCEPTIVE WELLNESS

Studio Prix

1. How can architecture and urban intervention engage in human sensory perception so that new or nuanced affects are produced providing alternative perspectives on our environment and condition?

2. Can spatial and functional conditions be tuned to provoke new understandings of the human condition – a perceptive wellness program?

Bad Vienna is a transitory programmed space that interrupts the expected city landscape, manipulates spatial affect and challenges known boundaries of public and private space with the intention of manipulating sensory perception. The architecture of Bad Vienna combines program, circulation and enclosure in a treatment of spatial perceptive effects including simultaneity, blurriness, light modulation, material variation, porosity, and disorientation to exploit and question the relationships between physical and perceptive space.

Simultaneity
Programmed pedestrian exhibition promenade. Bridge connection between 1st and 2nd district. User moves up and down through the space experiencing the exhibition promenade and simultaneously having a visual connection to the bath activities: bubble capsules, steam bar, hot pool, summer pool, etc.

Blurriness
Moving through the environment inside and outside spaces are not defined. This in-between space condition creates disorientation.

Light/material/porosity
Light conditions change through the use of irregular envelope apertures (vertical louvers) creating different shadow/light effects/conditions and transparencies/opacities.

Location disorientation
The use of scattered configurations of envelope apertures and two circulation systems that continuously loop blurs your perception of location within the building and the city. It creates a labyrinth like feeling of walking through the building. Nonetheless, the apertures have views toward city landmarks that allow you to somehow recognize your location within the city.

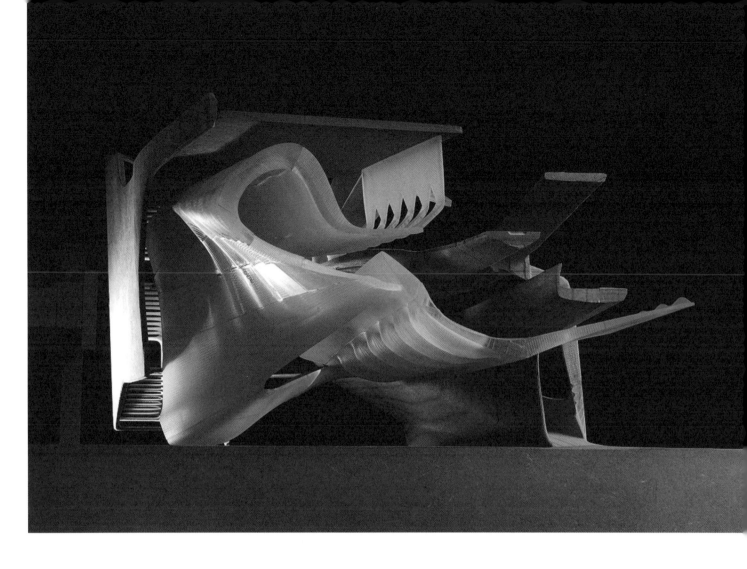

Nora Graw

ANIMATED ATMOSPHERE

Studio Lynn

Whereas live-action films must either restrict themselves to the material conditions of the film set or collage in artificial surroundings, animated films are free to create complete abstract environments that extract and exaggerate qualities of the physical world. These environmental choices are invariably atmospheric and aesthetic and work like an all-around version of the sliding backdrop scenery of a theatrical production. This project, located in the Puerto Madero arts district in Buenos Aires, creates a single incubating workplace for independent animated filmmakers. At the urban scale these upcoming designers are given a collective identity through a more homogeneous exterior; however, once inside the building the architecture transitions to a heterogeneous and spatial complex interior capable of supporting the diverse talent contained within.

The project creates a rich environment that draws from the tradition of coulisse layering. Such layering interconnects diverse stage settings with "real world" players. In this project such interconnection is fashioned with a system of thin surface layers that produce both the cohesive, iconic exterior and the multilayered permeable interior. These surfaces are imprinted with conditions such as structure, ornament and shading that transform continuously through blends and superimpositions that create a diverse set of internal scenes and strong perspectives with spatial depth. These layers also merge and separate to reveal different surface qualities and organize space.

The building accommodates several large volumes – a film screening theatre, exhibition space and entertainment hall – that act as programmatic attractors for the public and highlight the smaller businesses and enhance their connection to the film industry. Shared spatial program-matic elements such as combinable offices, conference rooms and editing facilities allow diverse groups to organize, aggregate and form clusters as projects and opportunities materialize.

Julia Körner

SUPERHUMAN ENTICEMENT

Studio Lynn

Superhuman Enticement is a new showroom, manufacturing and therapy building catering to clients of advanced prosthetic and biomechatronic devices. Unlike traditional prosthetics, Biomechatronic engineering integrates living tissue with synthetic components to produce seamless and often superhuman performance.

This project creates an architectural identity for the evolutionary, futuristic lifestyle of the contemporary amputee; a lifestyle celebrating a mysterious synthesis of organic body and technology. My architecture creates similarly enigmatic effects through the fusion of landscape, highly articulated volumes and a luminous, gravity defying roof. Synthesizing the aesthetics of humanoid robot design and a wooded forest, my project animates the smooth, clean and continuous surfaces of the building volumes with constantly changing light and shadow patterns produced by a space frame roof structure. This highly designed ambiance fully fuses and transforms the therapy, factory and showroom building typologies into a continuously shifting field of sophisticated, highly-differentiated architectural moments. These moments produce effects that echo the recent startling advances Biomechatronics.

Project Design

Located in Manhattan, the project occupies an existing pier in the East River near the Manhattan Bridge. The building is a full-service Prosthetics-Biomechatronic Device dealership consisting of a large showroom for display, zones for light manufacturing and fitting and therapy areas for clients. A continuous sports landscape for physical training slips in and out of the building and covers the entire surface of the pier.

The building consists of three primary systems: the ground, the volumes and the roof. These systems work together to control the flow of circulation on the site and create the architectural language of the project. The shapes of the volumes and the flowing patterns of the roof structure and landscape create an architecture of fluid movement and speed. Walking through the project, over ramps and through the building, clients experience enigmatic spatial effects as motion is communicated through formally different geometries that are still part of a single organic family.

The primary space of the project is the central hall, a space that is created and activated by roof, ground and adjacent volumes. This space is large, continuous and functionally diverse. Clients arrive in this space and may examine the latest products in the showroom. From here they enter the organically shaped, nested volumes that border on the hall. It is within these volumes that clients are examined and fitted with their prosthetics.

Additional volumes hold physical therapy spaces, fabrication, clinical and administrative design spaces. The surfaces of these volumes make enclosure – walls and floors – as well as ramps and paths that ensure the continuity of athletic movement through the factory and retail spaces.

On top of the volumes floats a large, three-dimensional space frame roof that creates a ceiling producing shadow and lighting effects through the day. This roof – a technological magic carpet covering the entire building – uses the organic volumes as columns and forms a nested roof space poché relationship to the surface of them where they connect.

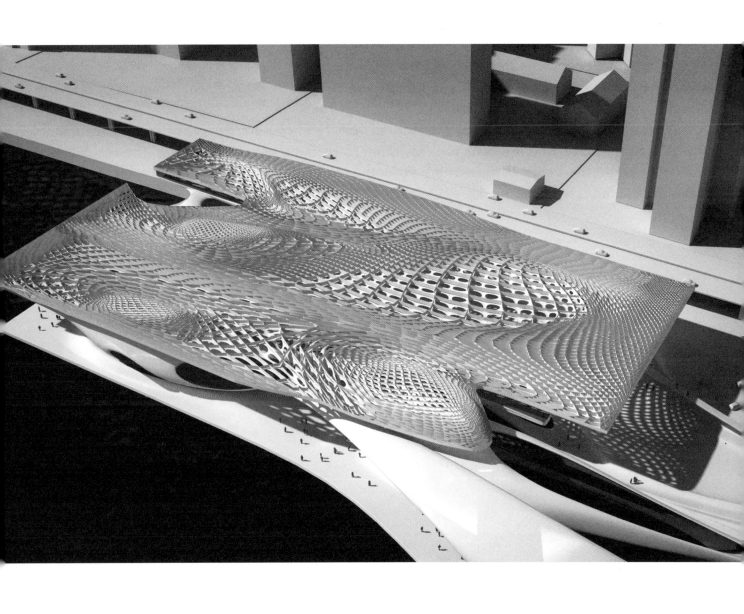

Quirin Krumbholz

IDEA NODE

Studio Prix

The Idea Node is a conceptual think tank stemming from the original program from the Chicago Square competition in Hamburg in 2006. It interconnects the diverse functional aspects of a city with a public parliamentary role-play to investigate social and economical positions apart from lobbying and commercial dependencies.

The urban design strings the broad functional variety of commercial areas, offices, residential spaces, a hotel, parks and the think tank together to create a new iconic figure. The result is an open networked landmark at the eastern tip of the Hafen City Hamburg defining the new gate to the city center.

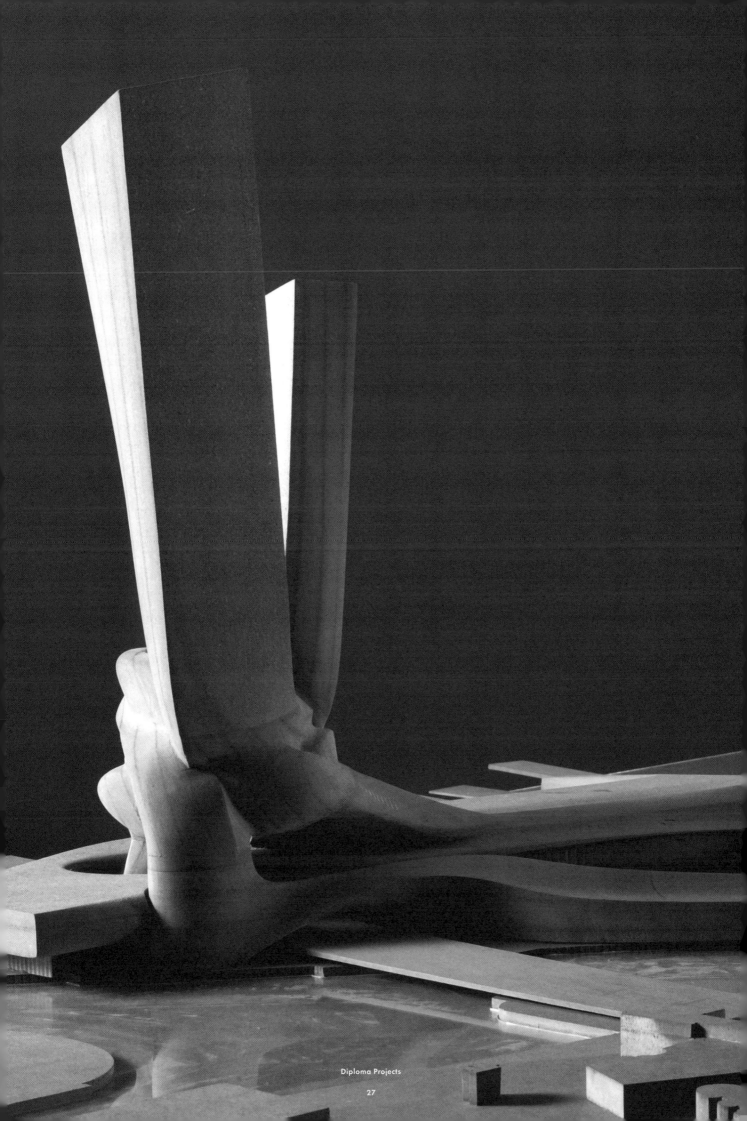

Jiri Matura

ROBOTICS TECHNOLOGY RESEARCH INSTITUTE

Studio Lynn

The Robotics Technology Research Institute, located on Barcelona's Avinguda Diagonal, is striving to become an integral part of the Area@22 technology corridor. The goal of this district is to support innovation in the fields of information, communications and media technologies, medical science and energy. The building, situated on a central site in this area, creates a direct and potentially transformative interdisciplinary link between these enterprises through the introduction of cutting-edge robotics technology. The central objective of the project is to create a formal response to the changing nature of contemporary research which now often operates in the overlapping realms of industry, academia, art and the public. Architecturally, this shift requires a new approach to the laboratory-factory building.

My building negotiates a triangular site and places the main entry into the volume on the urban corner, while the opposite side of the building merges continuously from the interior to the landscape. As an urban strategy, the project uses linear laminated surfaces to create continuous vectors from exterior to interior. To create enclosure and ground, these elements are strategically interrupted by surfaces which break their direction and deform to create building skin and a continuous landscape. On the interior, the linear elements delaminate, cross and interconnect intricately to serve as visual communicators, structure and circulation while also displacing a large volume in the center of the mass, transforming the void space into a horizontal atrium. It is here that the project also works as a prototype for future projects. Its complex, networked interior transforms the typical the atrium building typology into an animated, central exhibition void. This shared, flexible space works as a connective tissue that both represents and amplifies the relationship inbetween the three realms of robotics innovation: research, development and mass communication.

This project creates a dynamic setting for research, a place where public interaction plays an important role in the transmission of information between end-user and creator. The building physically opens itself to the public through curated exhibition space and direct circulation paths that provide dynamic views of work-in-progress. Ultimately, the building's configuration allows for near-instantaneous feedback between design teams and end users, creating more seamless incorporations of the design adaptations needed for innovation.

Peter Mitterer

NEW BOUWKUNDE DELFT

Studio Hadid

Situated in between Delft's historic city centre and the campus of the Technical University, New Bouwkunde Delft proposes a replacement for the burnt-down faculty of architecture. The project aims at substituting the traditional binary circulation logic of educational buildings for a highly differentiated network logic.

Representational spaces and those for production are accordingly split into linear strings and flexible, nonlinear pockets. The areas of intersection between levels and strings are envisioned to become hybrids of circulatory elements and public functions, resulting in a maximization of possible social and creative interaction.

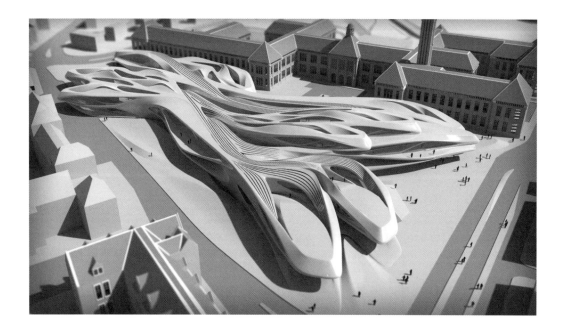

Diploma Projects

Philipp Ostermaier

TAIPEI 810° THEATRE

Studio Hadid

The diploma project Taipei 810° is based on a competition brief for a performing arts venue in Taipei, Taiwan. The brief asks for a cohesive overall design, which encompasses three theatres in a single building.

After researching different theatre typologies with a strong focus on the relation between audience and stage, a basic common formula for the aforementioned stages emerged: A 180° opera, 270° thrust stage theatre and a 360° theatre in the round form the heart of the proposed scheme. As means of cohering the different typologies into the required single envelope, the project exploits the parametric malleability of delaminating shell surfaces as primary design tool, making them at the same time read as individual units but also recognizable as part of a whole.

On an urban level the project seeks to integrate the surrounding urban fabric, lifting its main volume from the ground in order to allow local pedestrian traffic to flow freely between the individual theatres. The generated urban pathways gradually become part of the theatres' main lobbies before they emerge on top of the building as part of the undulating roof structure, which therefore becomes an extension of the public space.

Maja Ozvaldic

INSIDE OUT

Studio Lynn

This project is a new performing art center for the Portuguese city of Guimarães, a European Capital of Culture in 2012. Once designated by the EU, a Capital of Culture city is given a period of one year to showcase its cultural life and development. A number of European cities have used this program to transform their cultural base and, in doing so, the way in which they are viewed internationally. With the aim of arousing citizens' interest and facilitating the long-term cultural development of the city, projects are undertaken to restore local heritage and to create new facilities to generate steady cultural growth and flourishing cultural tourism.

This project is concerned with architecture and urban development as initiators of significant cultural evolution, a process capable of transforming both societal and city structures. With this goal in mind, this performing arts center aims to capitalize on the Capital of Culture phenomenon through a strategy of "acupuncture urbanism", revitalizing an unexploited part of the city by seeding it with a critical attractor for future cultural development. To accomplish this, this project both respects the scale of the existing neighborhood while also drawing it into a radically new and seductive zone of cultural transformation.

Architecturally, my main interest is the generation of an enticing exterior public space with an interior atmosphere. This space is designed as a continuous "outdoor ballroom" that branches out and inserts itself between the building's key volumes and draws the public in from the perimeter. Programmatically the ballroom courtyard works as a performance area that can, depending on the event, also serve as a covered outdoor lobby for the project's theatre, auditorium, exhibition space and classroom areas. These aspects of the program are housed in four volumes distributed on the site to shape and emphasize the central void of the exterior ballroom. These volumes, echoing scale of the surrounding neighborhood, also form an enclosing system which follows the perimeter of the site and creates a continuous, decisive edge. From the street the building appears as one introverted entity.

Both systems – the volumes and the ballroom – share the same structural principle of a steel egg-crate. This structure is more expressed in the second system where it articulates the courtyard's façade and roof-like shading system. The exterior surfaces of the volumes are clad with ceramic panels. In the passage area the same materials with different shades of white (from white to gray) are used. The project's main atmospheric effect – a filtered luminosity – is created by the way light and shadow interact with this surface gradient through the egg-crate.

Maria-Helene Pollhammer

AYURVEDA CENTER AUSTRIA

Studio Lynn

The Indian method of alternative medicine known as Ayurveda is approximately 3000 years old and concentrates on a philosophy of living. Within this system yoga, meditation and nutrition are important methods of treatment for finding balance in life. The traditional setup of an Ayurveda clinic originates in Far Eastern culture and is inspired by its traditions and history. My project reinterprets the pavilion typology to create a new Ayurveda Center for Austria. Small intimate structures and huts are organized along a pristine natural lake near Salzburg in tune with the alpine environment. Through careful design the project fuses the existing Asian healing technique with a Western milieu and creates the base for an unsurpassed contemporary, global treatment center.

The overall ambience of the building is characterized by a reduced, almost minimal, environment crafted from continuous surfaces. Soft glowing light and the subtle texture of the building surfaces reinforce the therapeutic mission of the architecture. The project's organization is guided by a strong sense of public and private areas. Spatial zones vary from an expansive, multi-level public entry to the intimate and remote pavilions facing Hintersee Lake. The building also reacts to and interacts with the rugged alpine terrain of the site. The project begins with a strong gesture, a small, multi-storey hotel near the entry, and gradually dissolves into the landscape. Along the lakefront, the branching system of the pavilions assembles different spatial hierarchies and creates infinite loops of circulation and multiple perspectives to the exterior. This puts focus on the inhabitants themselves who are encouraged to turn their attention to the surrounding natural environment.

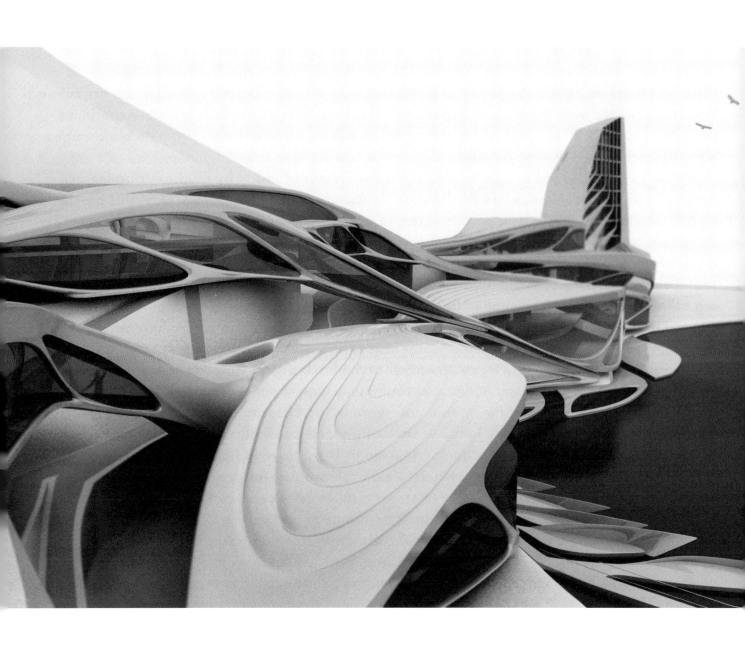

Anna Psenicka

DIAPHANOUS

Studio Lynn

The urban life of Paris dramatically changed with the introduction of the passage. Far from simple shopping arcades, the Parisian passage created an icon for the city and a destination for the flaneur to enjoy abandon and luxury in a disorienting, new urban landscape – one filled with unprecedented moods of light and the temptation to look at the diversity of things and observe others doing the same. Attitudes fostered by the original arcades are still central cultural values associated with the sensual experience of urban life in Paris. Such sensual experience has been partially threatened and undermined by the subsequent transformation of passages into straightforward shopping malls.

My interest is to establish new territories for the flaneur of today by reintroducing the ambience of the diaphanous into the Parisian landscape in a contemporary way. This project embraces the diaphanous as a porous structure, permeable for light and air, which creates numerous possibilities for vistas and perceptions within and without. The building aims to create a prototypic situation of densification and new icon for the city; one that creates a destination that gives more features to the urban space by extending the street level into the air and engaging adjacent buildings. By elevating the building from the street level to the roof level, the ground is almost untouched but modulated from above. This creates a new relationship between the observer underneath the roof, the visitor inside the structure and the city itself.

The project is located at the Place Baudoyer at the back side of Hotel de Ville in Paris. It creates a dynamic new canopy building to roof an existing street, two plazas with cafes and a well-used market, and part of the interior courtyard of the Caserne Napoléon, soon to be refurbished to connect to the city hall. To convincingly and poetically cover these diverse urban conditions, a system of gradually changing elements is employed to adapt to the needs of a long-span structure with both porosity and inhabitable spaces. This system is composed from structural modules that have the ability to create a multiplicity of spatial conditions, interweave inside and outside zones and be porous both horizontally and vertically. Structurally the modules create simple arches – creased steel plates with ribs – aggregated into pockets. Taking examples from the history of long-span structures, this module is designed to mutate from vaulted surfaces into a space frame. This gradient transformation, from space pockets to porous structure, also creates a system of openings that erodes the edges of the building. Atmospherically, the core effect of the canopy building is one of an artificial nature that works to filter sunlight during day and emit glowing light at night.

Visible from the Seine and spanning Rue Rivoli, the building creates a destination that also functions as a progressive icon for the neighbourhood. Also from an urban standpoint, the roof extends and deepens the use of the existing plazas, enabling them to work as a more permanent food market while also adding leisure and cultural facilities, such as a bistro connected to the market, a cafe, a cafe-theatre and an outdoor amphitheatre in the courtyard of the Caserne. By concentrating diverse program within a single, elegant structure that works in tandem with existing features of the plazas, the site should be transformed into an energetic urban hub, activated day and night.

Saman Saffarian

CHICAGO TRAIN STATION 2020

Studio Hadid

The project proposes a new train station on a site located in the center of Chicago city. It envisions the undulating roof structure of the station to form an urban park, from which the tracks below can easily be accessed. Accordingly, the diploma focuses on the development of the station roof as key element of the design, elaborating it as a porous structure which can assume a wide variety of different states: From opaque shelter to translucent textile, operable roof to highly articulate park-scape. In order to achieve as wide a range of different affects /effects as possible the design deploys a parametric design model by setting up associative rules for the adaptively interacting subsystems.

Bengt Stiller

PIERCING GLANCE

Studio Lynn

Piercing Glance: A stacked vertical piazza, organized around a central atrium to encourage social interest in New Media Technologies.

Piercing Glance, a New Media Center in Paris, aspires to manifest the importance of new media technologies and their ubiquity in our everyday life. The building aims to challenge the enclosed, bunker-like typology of a storage space – holding digital data – with a light-flooded, vibrant vertical plaza that accommodates different kinds of exhibition spaces and allows insight into the machine behind it.

A vertical piazza – the central space for informal social, intellectual and creative exchange – forms the heart of the New Media Center. Major escalators ascend eight stories from the ground level through the sky-lit central atrium, which itself extends to the full height of the building. This vertical piazza is the heart of the building, connecting meeting places, sky lobbies, a restaurant, exhibition spaces and a two-hundred-seat auditorium.

In the spirit of the world wide web-based quest for free, open and accessible data, the building itself is symbolically open to the city. Visual transparencies and accessible public spaces connect the tower to the physical, social and cultural fabric of its urban context. At street level, a molded plaza with a half-way covered pathway invites the neighborhood to observe and take part in the activity contained within. A cafeteria, an exhibition gallery for temporary installations and small shops are easily accessible public functions placed at the levels −1 to +2.

Responding to its urban context, the sculpted façade establishes a distinctive identity for Bastille Square. The building's corner entry is elevated to draw people into the lobby in a deferential gesture towards its neighbors. The façade registers the iconic, curving profile of the central atrium as a glazed figure which appears to be carved out of a monolithic block, connecting the vibrant activity of the central atrium to the city.

Milan Suchanek

PUBLIC LIBRARY IN OSLO

Studio Hadid

The project of the public library in Oslo is based on three main topics.
- The position and image of the library in current cultural situation
- Research on typology of the library
- Surface articulation in accordance with inner and outer influences

The functions of a library have changed dramatically in the last years. The image of knowledge and information "tank" does not work any more. It is becoming to be much more an cultural and social meeting point. The formal and ideological integration in the city or another social community is necessary.

For this reason the entire volume is split into the smaller pavilion-like units. The low height of these components, accessible surfaces, integration under the ground and the connection with the existing water surface based on the "figure ground principle" offers a connection with the urban situation. On this principle arises a gradient between positive and negative geometries with integrated pedestrian walks which suppose to create an urban kind of feeling inside of this structure.

The functional organization is driven by the differentiation of the privacy within the library. There are three basic levels and six types of library units. The combination between these variables allows to achieve different situations and types of spaces. From introverted negative geometries to positive open spaces. The books are distributed over the delivery points which are situated in the nodes between the library units. The technology of a rapid delivery system which was first used in the cargo industry allows independent distribution of books in the entire library.

The last but very important point of the research was the articulation of the surface. There are three basic inputs:
- Light exposure
- Accessibility
- Structural thickness

All these inputs are based on the research on patterns and possibilities of merging different types of patterns, structural characteristics of these patterns and the computional analysis of developed geometry driven by light exposure as well as the urban situation.

The final result is an overlay of these inputs.

The surface geometry is based on a component kind of logic. This method allows one to handle the ornament, structural thickness as well as the porosity of the surfaces. In the second procedure populated components react to each other in accordance with outer influences. This experiment increases the number of variables and a certain design flexibility enormously.

The integration of these main topics in the hierarchy of the project and the methodology of design process driven by computational technologies (scripting and prototyping) were the crucial points of the project.

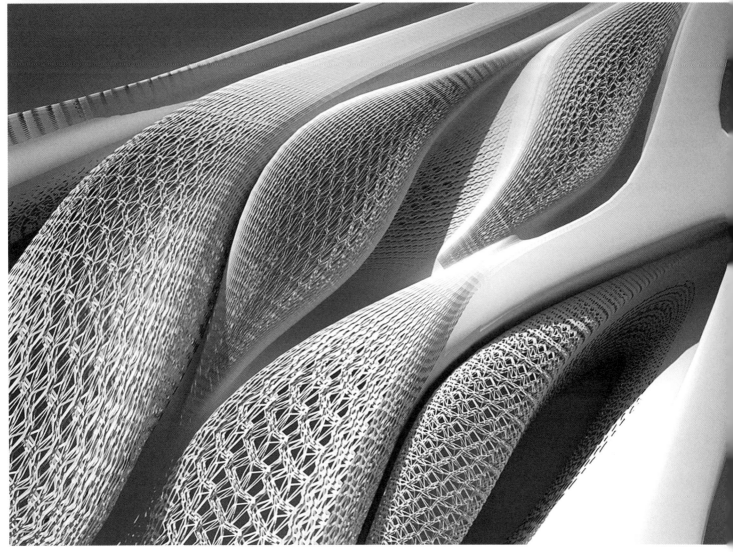

Florian von Hayek

CERN RESEARCH CENTER, GENEVA

Studio Lynn

The project generates an atmosphere of permanently linked and networked exchange of knowledge within a building dedicated to science and research. The building seeks to highlight the most important initial item of CERN, the Large Hadron Collider (LHC) Tunnel. The tunnel both physically represents the scientific work within the building and is utilized to translate science into an architectural language.

In the past research buildings have often been detached from architectural issues and have have come to resemble generic office buildings. Historically science and research facilities derive from rather elitist typologies like monasteries and, later, university campuses, which many contemporary projects still refer to. Today, especially at CERN, science distributes knowledge throughout the world, by means of the internet, making it more accessible and reaching far beyond the scientific field.

In contrast to the typology of the monastery, this project is conceived as a publicly accessible building which embraces intersections, creating spatial interfaces that both visually connect and physically separate space.

Based on the rules of particle interaction, this project aims to translate this interaction into architecture. Gravity and lightness control the relationship of the building to the ground, through carving, as well as the relation of the ground to the sky. Using the principles of magnetic forces that attract and repel depending on the charge, the program separates building functions, such as public exhibition spaces and intimate research spaces. This detachment of program creates voids and intersections that result in a dynamic interface between the two types of program, ultimately inhabited by the conference center and the shared library/media center.

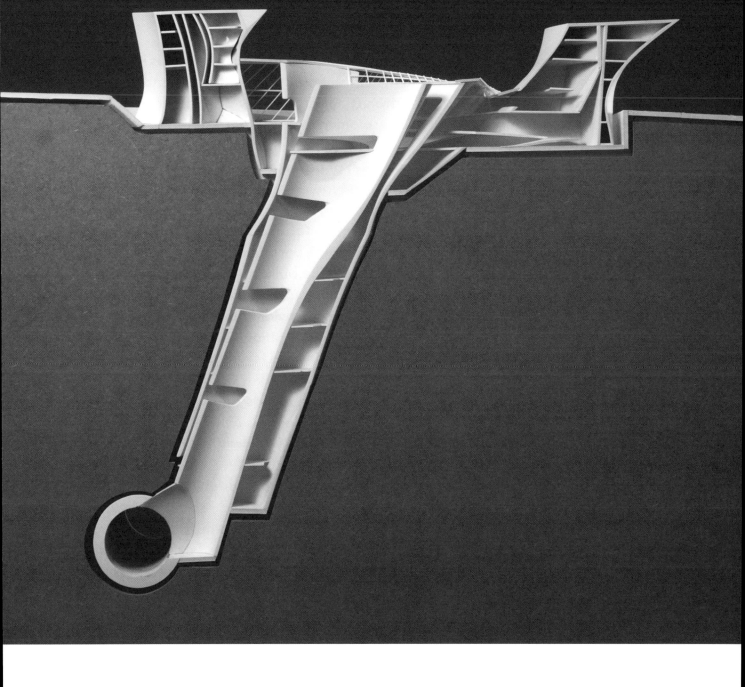

Adam Vukmanov

BIONOMIC PRECIPITOUSNESS

Studio Lynn

The diploma project reaches beyond the point of sustainable architecture as it is introduced today. It develops the architectural impact, beyond the current practice of attached and alienated building applications. The design of this high-rise project deals with new parametric design processes, established as "Bionomic Precipitousness" or ecologically driven perpendicular structure.

The data from domestic environmental elements such as wind and sun are combined with the functional organization of a building to create a set of parameters that generate a modeling base condition for a new "zero + energy" high-rise typology. The result is a vertical, voluptuous pattern on the city horizon with a diverse structural sub-matrix that reacts on multiple scales. In relation to the rhythm of the old urban fabric of Zagreb, Croatia, the tower is an anomaly within the city block. It appears differently from each viewpoint, becoming a significant landmark in the mixed context of historic and modern architecture. On the building scale, the project varies in all directions, creating unique interior and exterior spatial scenarios. The interior volumes fluctuate and correspond to the façade distortions on every floor, providing diverse horizon views.

The main ecological high-performance system is the integration of natural ventilation within the geometry of the building façade. The processed air is used for heating in the winter and cooling in the summer. Due to this design feature, the tower avoids using artificial air conditioning systems. Natural air is drawn into the building through façade openings and moves within the building skin. Depending on the time of year, the outside air is either cooled by collected gray water or heated through sun exposure. The air ultimately enters the interior spaces and exists through designed voids, completing the cycle.

Deformation and differentiation of the façade is generated by designing the air intakes based on the height-pressure difference of the air. The double skin shifts and reacts depending on sun exposure, including direction and angle. It also takes into account the behavior and angle of the wind/air stream on the exterior surface which is precisely calculated using computer-fluid-dynamic software. Finally, the building corresponds and mutates based on the direct relationship of the buildings functions, performance requirements and the structural distribution of the vertical load through the massive cores and open voids.

Diploma Projects

Aurelius Weber

BROADCASTING STATION FOR ROME

Studio Lynn

The building is a composition of different modules which interact to develop a system which works as a connector in an aesthetical and structural sense. The three-dimensional pattern on the façade adapts according to its position and function. Along with integrated structure the building skin provides a shading system capable of reacting at any "moment" to the light exposure. The diverse programmatic mix of a broadcasting station provides an opportune scenario for developing the relationship between inside and outside.

Philipp Weisz

BROOKLYN ARTS TOWER

Studio Hadid

The project is based on a competition in the center of Brooklyn, in the BAM_cultural district and provides a strategy for flipping mixed-use urban programs, consisting of an outdoor theater (−15 m), a bam_theater (+30 m), a performance space (+120 m), galleries, ateliers, commercial space, and private areas, as residential and office parts, into a compressed complex verticality. Because the site is surrounded by lots of cultural institutes, it was the aim of the project to create a gate for this highly developed cultural area, producing perceptional iconic views through the building's geometry, as well as through façade effects. By using structural and programmatic slices, instead of a typical static core, the tower provides massive voids and views in the inside, and thus reflects its mixed use program on a noticeable vertical broadway.

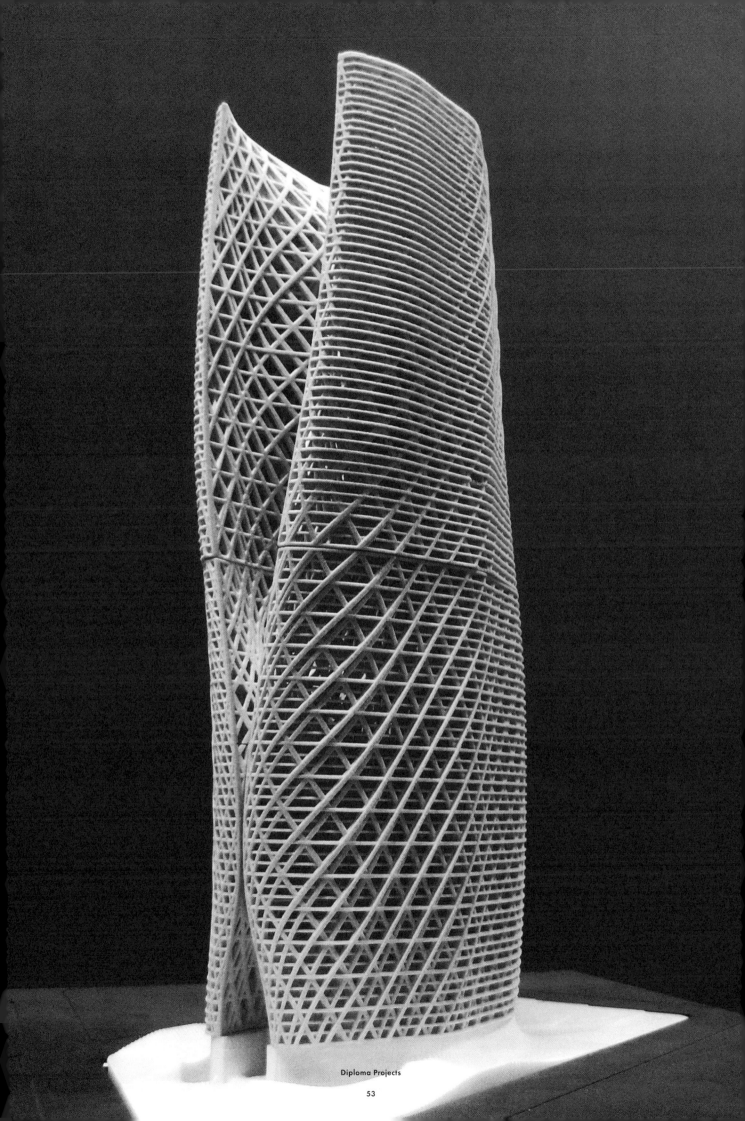

Diploma Projects

Rupert Zallmann

SUBSTITUTE MATRIX

Studio Prix

The substitute matrix is a system which as the first step registers data, from the site and the given functional requirements, two-dimensionally into a spreadsheet where they are analyzed and reorganized. The format of the spreadsheet resembles the undistorted and unrolled volume of the building. The processed data is translated directly into spatial elements and addressed to the site. The driving parameters of the matrix for this specific "case study" building are climate control, lighting, functional densities, structural properties and circulation requirements. Hence the appearance and the spatial complexity of the building, is not designed but depends merely on the overlay of different layers of variable numeric information.

Case Study: Catch Club
Site: Wiener Eislaufverein, Vienna
Program: Ice-skating rink, wrestling arena, hotel, retail, recreation

DESIGN STUDIOS

STUDIO HADID

Photo: Simone Cecchetti

<u>Head</u>
Prof. Zaha M. Hadid

<u>Assistant Professors</u>
Christian Kronaus
Jens Mehlan
Johann Traupmann
Mascha Veech

<u>Lecturers</u>
Robert Neumayr-Beelitz
Patrik Schumacher
Jan Tabor

<u>Organization</u>
Susanne John

Architecture is a design discipline that is always confronted with new design tasks. It searches for new solutions for already known design tasks. It is the expression of continuous advancement in given social challenges as well as the conceptual, formal and methodological means of coping with these challenges.

Studying architecture means first of all acquiring conceptual, methodological and formal resources for coping with various design challenges. It is important to acquire a broad repertoire of design resources. They can only be acquired by trying out concepts, design methods and forms. The "academic" challenges lend themselves especially well to this acquisition of concepts, forms and work methods.

This method of teaching architecturehas its roots beyond a classical typologically oriented architectural teaching. It allows the development of a new "architectural language" that enables one to cope with new architectural challenges. Possible form generating processes are worked out in interdisciplinary and interconceptual debates and translated into a "new architectural language."

Development of the design project is carried out in small groups of two to three students, who work together on the task for one semester.

Ali Rahim

INTERIORITIES

Interiorities

Cultural and technological innovations establish new status quos and updated platforms from which to operate and launch further innovations to stay ahead of cultural developments. Design research practices continually reinvent themselves and the techniques they use, and guide these innovations to stay ahead of such developments. Reinvention can come through techniques that have already been set in motion, such as dynamic systems and other open source software programs that are mined for all their potential, through the development of new plug-ins that are able to change attributes within dynamic systems, or through changing existing or writing new expressions in the form of scripts in computer language – in effect changing the capacity of the operation of the software to develop new techniques for the design and manufacture of architecture. These techniques are important to design research to inform the form, space and material conditions of architecture. All will continue to be developed and alter the way architectural practices operate in the near and long term. Practices can also develop new techniques by investigating new technologies on the horizon of other fields. The necessary characteristics of the technologies selected are that they contain feedback, are inter-relational and have the potential to destabilize their current contexts. Techniques borrowed from other spheres can assist architectural practices to become more synthetic, seamlessly integrating the design, testing and manufacture of material formations.

Beyond Techniques to Elegance

The development of techniques is essential for innovation in design. However, the mastering of techniques, whether in design, production or both, does not necessarily yield great architecture. In Studio Hadid, Interiorities: An Urban Club for New York City (spring 2009) was an attempt to move beyond techniques by mastering them to achieve nuances within a formal development of projects that exude an elegant aesthetic sensibility.

Architects who have been able to add such a layer of aesthetic sophistication to their designs share several characteristics that are key to current digital design discourse. All of their projects operate within emerging paradigms of generative techniques, and move past methods completely dependent on the rigorous application of scientific standards. Each exhibits a systemic logic of thought that eschews mapping a specific process, or revealing the process of an algorithm being generated, as strategies to generate a project's form. Instead, mastery of the techniques used allows each designer to assume a more sophisticated relationship with the creation of form – using malleable forms differentiated at varied rates that are correlated systemically – a position made possible only through the use of an aesthetic sensibility concomitant with a highly developed design ability.

Affective Formations: Interiorities

Architecture generates cultural change by intensifying and inflecting existing modes of inhabitation, participation, and use. To accomplish this, architecture must become more responsive, engaging in a relationship of mutual feedback with its users and contexts. In other words, it must contain *affects* – the capacity to both to affect and be affected. Affects differ from effects, which, in everyday parlance, imply a one-way direction of causality: a cause always precedes its intended effect. Affects, in contrast, suggest a two-way transfer of information and influence between a formation, or work of architecture, and its users and environment. While all works of architecture arguably have effects, certain projects are more prolific than others. In this design research studio we are interested in designing affective formations- works of architecture that maximize their affects and hence responsiveness to users and contexts.

Interiority suggests the focus on the creation of affective formations that unfold and differentiate within the terms of their own internal and perceptual logics. The creation of affects are most clearly pursued by starting with interiors, i.e. without immediately developing the architecture with an environment and exposing it to external influences such as gravity, environment, etc. Perceptual logics assist the way one experiences space and form when moving through and around the interiors. The creation of a series of optical illusions from different angles can be amplified developing a visual understanding of form that has a non-linear relationship to the actual geometry.

Studio Hadid was aiming to build up a multi-layered complexity with a high degree of differentiation within each visual system and scale with a high level of correlation between the various levels of perception. Each scale of internal differentiation is associated with corresponding or complementary differentiations within other scales. For example, nested scales of material/textural differentiation in relation to a continuous pattern in color variation allows for an elegant affect.

Methodology

Three primary trajectories for exploration were employed in developing the Urban Club for New York City:

1. Technique Development

Students in Hadid Studio used dynamical/generative techniques to understand and develop systemic logics that derive qualitative rates of change or velocity and quantitative amounts of change, such as direction, as well as accumulations and densities of formations. This interrelational software technology uses vectors of magnitude and direction that effect and accommodate threshold conditions of decay and transformation where the geometry of material relations exceeds the capacity for Gestalt definition. Some use these systems, or scripting, to map a scientific approach, or incorporate scientific rigor. The students used these systemic techniques to develop studies of the rate of change and enhance knowledge and understanding of formations. The development of this knowledge requires iteration, and through this iteration each student developed his or her own aesthetic sensibility.

2. Aesthetic Development

Each student team developed their own sensibility for variation using sub-division modeling techniques that were incorporated in the dynamical system using scripting techniques. The goal was to use extreme variation to produce unprecedented architectural effects that flow from surfaces, and part-to-part as well as part-to-whole arrangements in extreme variation to produce distinct formal features for interiorities with the morphological continuity to develop a building. The distinct features – soft to hard, for example – enabled the development of spaces with very disparate and discreet spatial, material and lighting qualities that begin to transform into each other to maintain morphological continuity. The projects able to produce the most radical differences with limits within an aesthetic sensibility were the most successful, the challenge always being to move away from component-based logics (which always produce part-to-part relationships) towards topological continuity that loses each part in the development of an entire project. The aesthetic development is crucial to transferring the emphasis of the design to the affects that it produces.

3. Project Developments and Location

The project was developed simultaneously with the development of aesthetic and technique. Students channeled and facilitated the design research towards an urban club located in the New York neighborhood of TriBeCa, on Varick Street between N Moore and Franklin Streets, between existing bars and bar/club hybrid typologies. The design focuses on a cluster of primary social rooms: lounge, dining room, library, conference room, ballroom and den. Intentionally very specific, it synthesizes all of these aspects without losing their intensity to create a complete architectural experience incorporating form, structure, material, texture, ornament, color, transparency/opacity and light and shadow.

The design research featured in Studio Hadid yields interesting knowledge in terms of how to turn a corner on the interior with material and the exterior with form, while the variation in color and lighting systems, as well as the control of part-to-part and part-to-whole relationships develop very specific atmospheres in different locations within each project. The spaces are different in scale, and the difference is exploited using material qualities, whether hard or soft, those are accentuated with color. The qualitative difference in each space and project is achieved through a transformation of spatial scale, material qualities, part-to-whole relationships, seaming pattern, lighting pattern and color accents that at the same time remain morphologically continuous. It is the high degree of variation that contributes to an environment that is able to develop the most qualitative difference in the morphological continuity of the project.

Studio project

INTERIORITIES

Winter term 2008/09

The notion of interiority suggests the elaboration of tectonic systems that unfold and differentiate within the terms of their own internal logic. This can be most clearly pursued if we start with interiors, i.e., without immediately placing the architecture into an environment and exposing it to external influences.

We are interested in developing complex, layered and highly differentiated tectonic systems that can start to compete with the best historical examples in terms of their richness, coherency and precision of formal organisation. We are aiming to reach the level of designed luxury we find, for instance, in the most filigree gothic spaces or the most excessive baroque or rococo interiors. And we aim to go beyond all known historical precedents in terms of qualitative differentiation and the intensity of part to part and part to whole relationships. Another way to express this is to say that we are aiming to build up a multi-layered complexity with a high degree of lawful differentiation within each system and with a high level of correlation between the various subsystems that constitute the overall tectonic system. Each subsystem as internal differentiation is associated with corresponding or complementary differentiations within the other subsystems. For example, structural differentiation is correlated with material/textural differentiation etc.

These ambitions are shared within contemporary avant-garde and constitute a clearly iden-tifiable style: parametricism. Like all avant-garde styles, parametricism can be characterized by its dogmas (positive heuristics) and taboos (negative heuristics) that give a clear a priori direction to the design research:
• Negative heuristics: avoid simple repetition of elements, avoid collage of unrelated elements.
• Positive heuristics: consider all forms to be parametrically malleable, differentiate gradually (at variant rates), correlate systematically.

As a brief to facilitate the design research towards a parametricist interiority we propose the design of an urban club in New York.

We are focussing our design effort on a cluster of primary social rooms: lounge, dining room, library, conference room, ballroom, den.

The design should synthesize all of the following registers or aspects that contribute to a full-blown architectural experience: form, structure, material, texture, ornament, colour, transparency/opacity, light/shadow.

The first task is to build up three "architectural surfaces" that are – each in their own way – characterized by a great range of internal differentiation. Each surface should be differentiated according to a qualitative opposition like hard/soft, light/heavy, etc. The next step is the development of each surface into a full enclosure. Then we can bring in programmatic concerns according to the brief. At this stage we are elaborating a system of performance-related morphological characters. In a further step we can start to establish a spatial order between the different rooms, and articulate connections and transitions. Then we work from the inside out in order to produce the external expression of the cluster. Finally, the whole complex is worked into and made to respond within an environment.

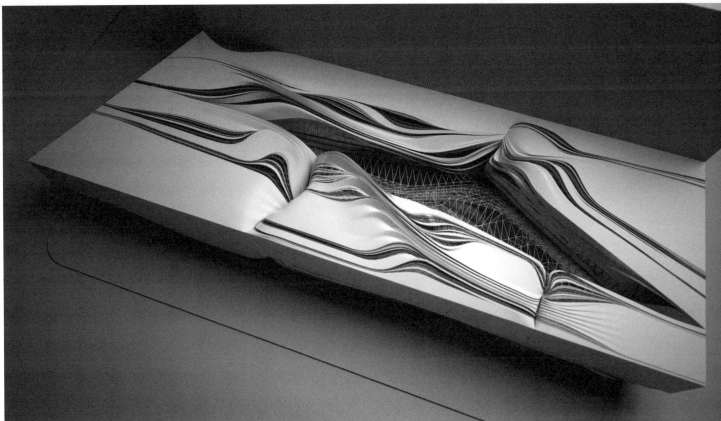

In-form, Krisztián Csémy, Jasmina Frincic, Jakub Klaska

Studio Hadid

Triangillo, Simon Emmanuel Aglas, Romina Hafner, Jakob Wilhelmstätter

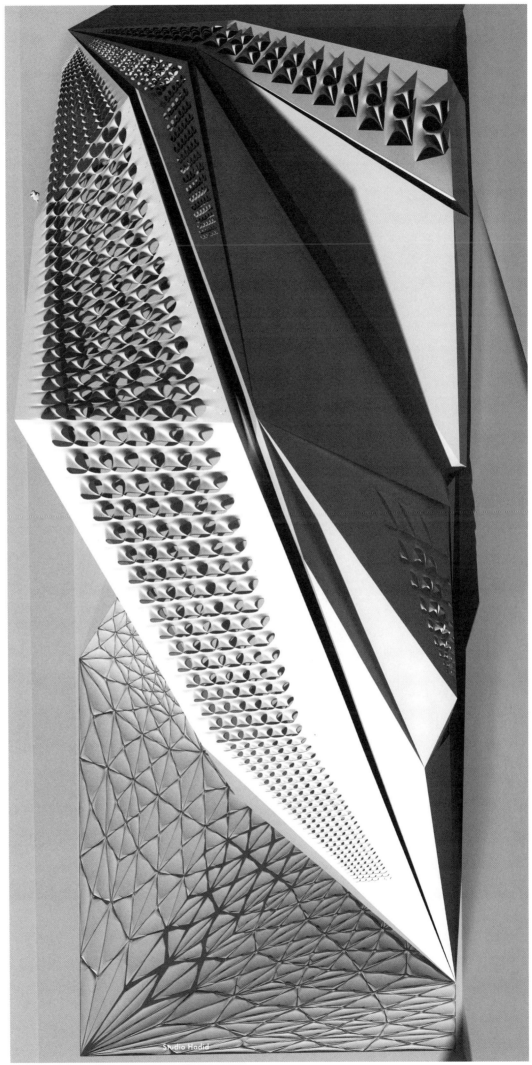

Triangillo, Simon Emmanuel Aglas,
Romina Hafner, Jakob Wilhelmstätter

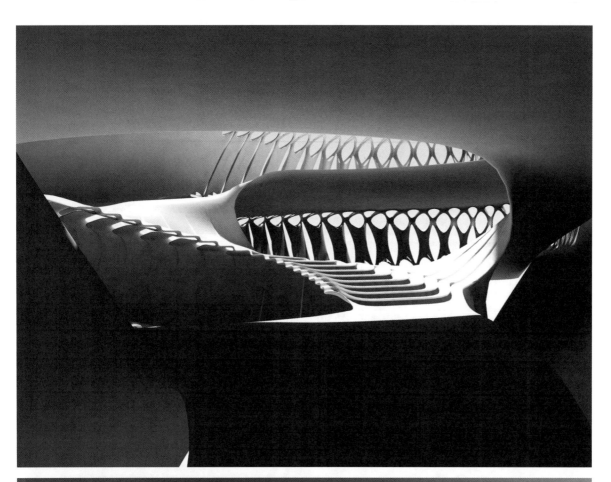

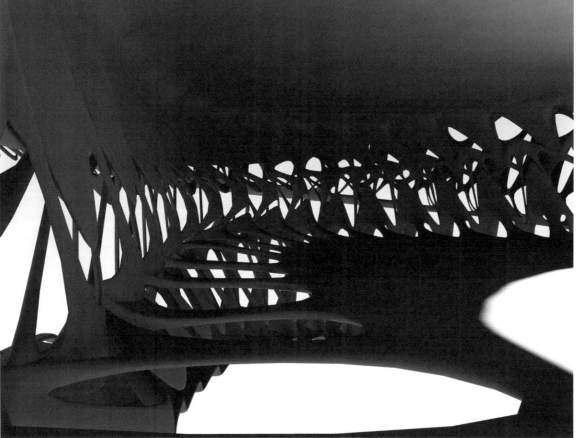

Surface Modulations, Manuel Fröschl, Maya Pindeus, Thomas Milly

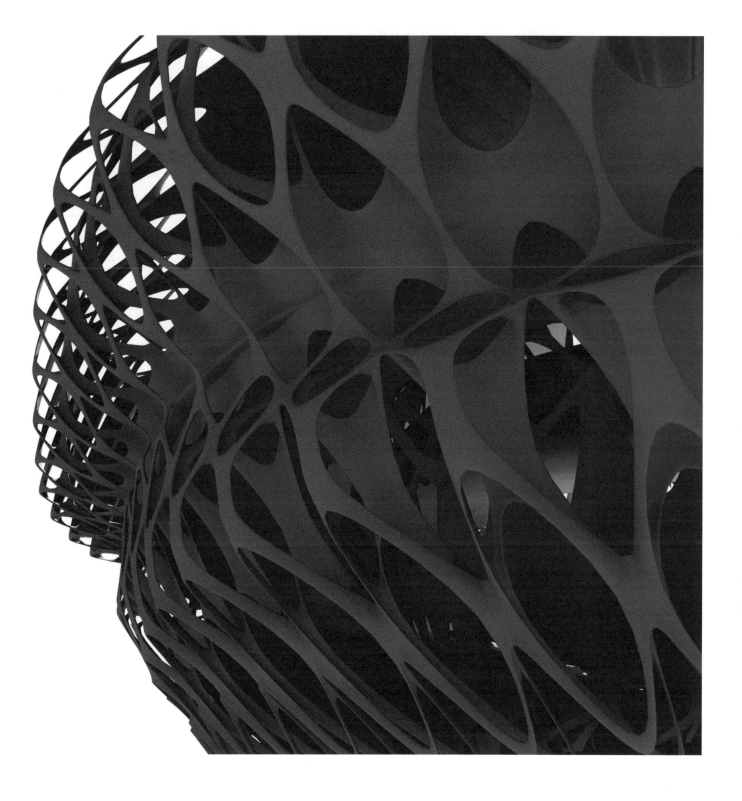

Surface Modulations, Manuel Fröschl, Maya Pindeus, Thomas Milly

Studio Hadid

Adaptive Grid, Philipp Hornung, Dimitri Tsiakas

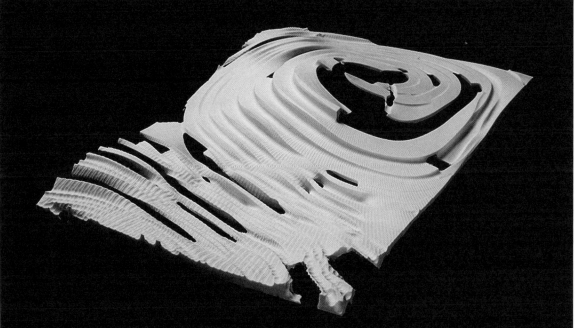

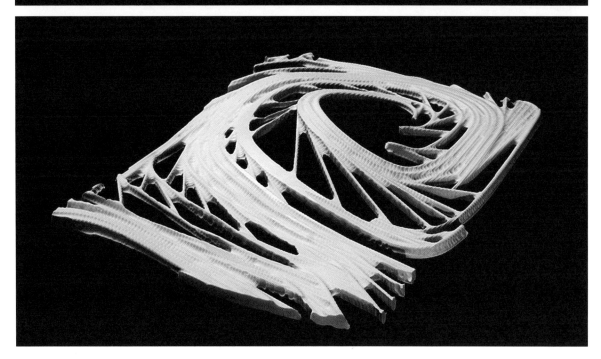

Barotic interiorities,
Roxelane Güllmeister,
Christoph Hermann,
Alexander Karaivanov,
Daniel Reist

Studio Hadid

INTERIORITIES 2

Summer term 2009

Continuing from the first semester, the main aim was to establish a multilayerd tectonic system that can operate on both, a small scale and as a supporting formwork with allows a seamless multifuntional integration into architectural interior.

We mainly focused on the differentiation between large structural elements and pure architectural elements and developed a cell structure wich reassembles them to form a continuous multidimensional network wich is able to create its own visual and functional aesthetics. Instead of using a system whose constitution is made of a composition of single elements we followed the idea of a system that generates its visual performance through its underlying function. Mathematical tesselations allows transitions from "structural" frameworks to be blended into more subtle surfaces without loosing its functional quality.

The interior can be seen as a collection of networks that shift between two and three dimensions, each creating their own unique visual characteristics reaching from random, more atmospheric conditions to large frameworks.

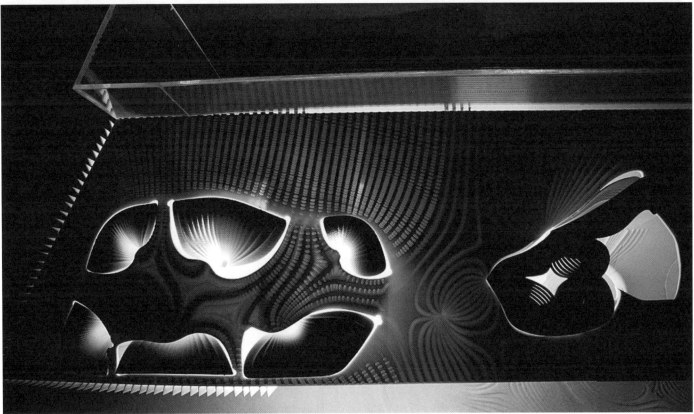

Barotic interiorities, Roxelane Güllmeister, Christoph Hermann, Alexander Karaivanov, Daniel Reist

Studio Hadid

Differelations, Kourosh Asgar-Irani, Josip Bajcer, Johannes Michael Bak, Marius Cernica

Design Studios

Element of Crime, Agnieszka Grochowska, Cornelia Klien, Magda Smolinska

Strandification, Niran Büyükköz, Martin Kleindienst, Raffael Petrovic

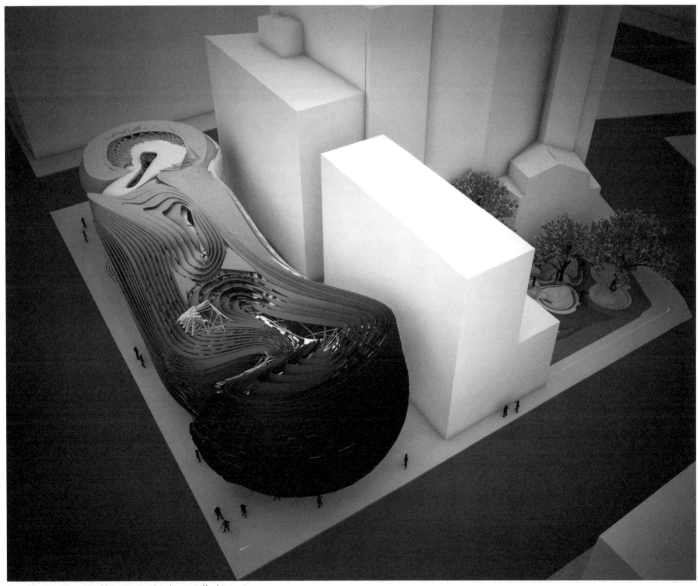

Strandification, Niran Büyükköz, Martin Kleindienst, Raffael Petrovic

Studio Hadid

Compo.ment.ics, Gilles Greis, Nikolay Ivanov

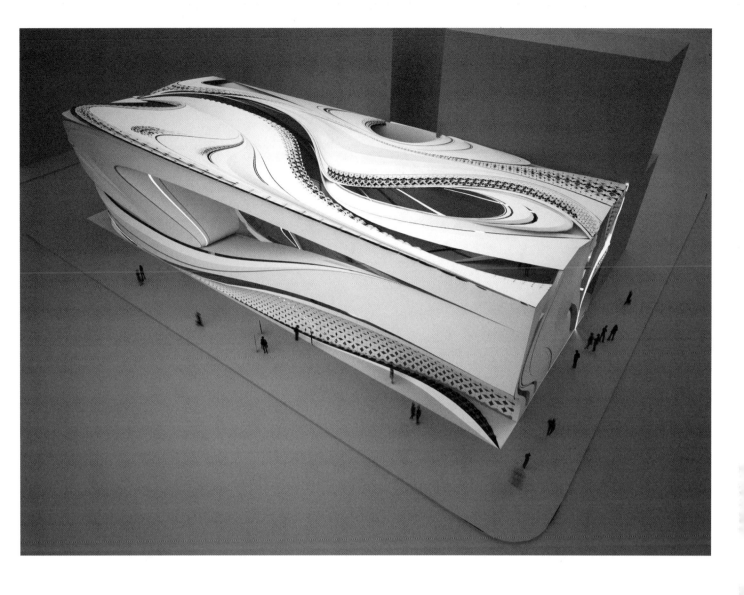

Compo.ment.ics, Gilles Greis, Nikolay Ivanov, Irina-Elena Preda

Studio Hadid

Delicious Collective, Seongheon Kim, Pop Sergiu-Radu, Dimitri Tsiakas

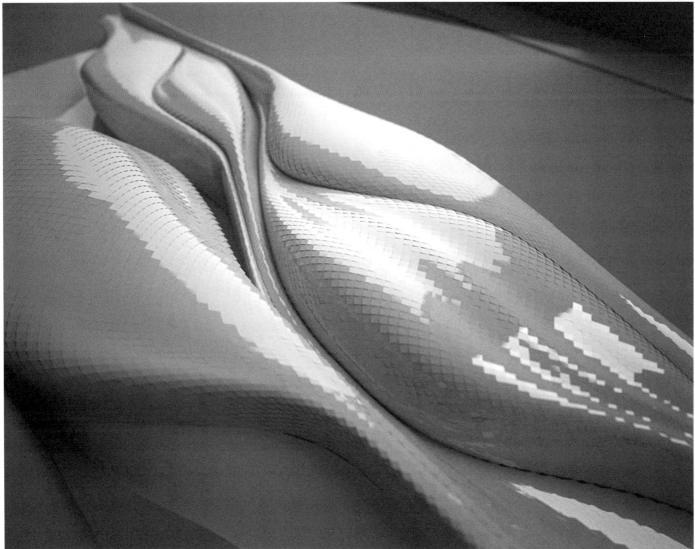

In-form, Krisztián Csémy, Jasmina Frincic, Jakub Klaska

Studio Hadid

Interiorities, Katharina Hieger, Galo Moncayo-Asan, Maya Pindeus

Design Studios

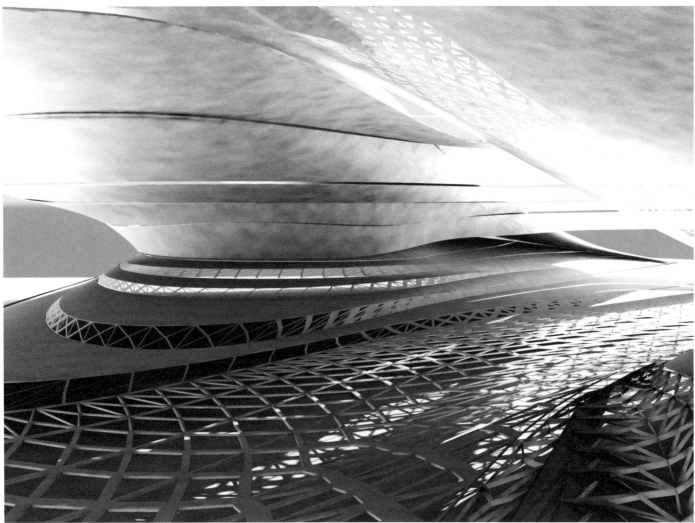

Interiority Intersection Urban Club, Na Bae Mi, Romina Hafner, Monir Karimi

Studio Hadid

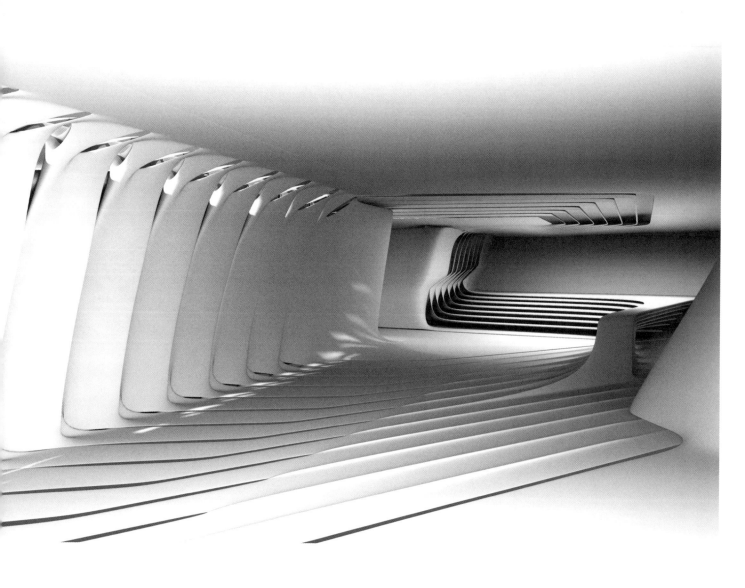

Interiorities Club New York, Manuel Fröschl, Sabrina Miletich

Tridensity, Simon Emmanuel Aglas, Philipp Hornung, Jakob Wilhelmstätter

Studio Hadid

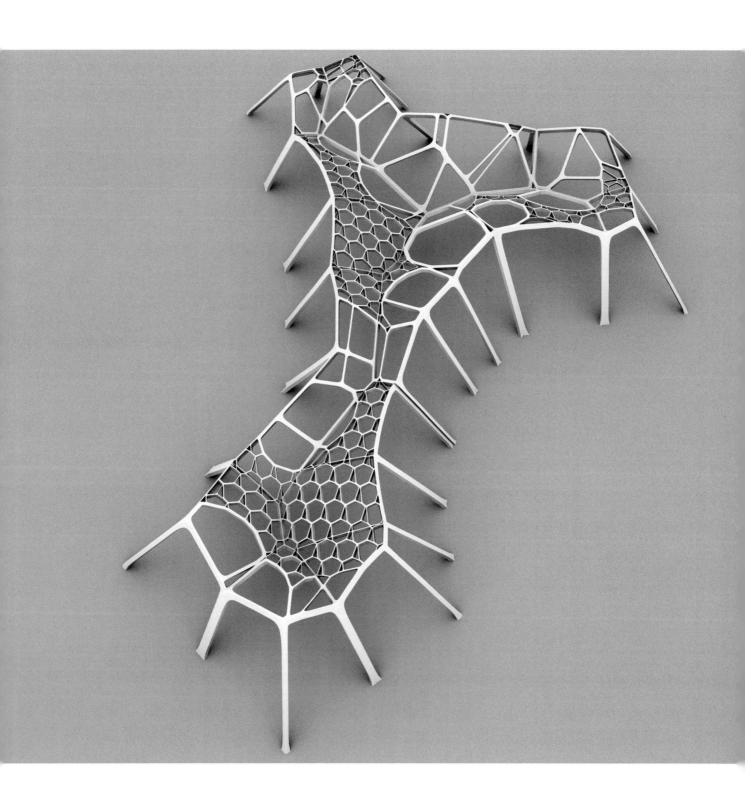

Porosity, Nicola Beck, Christoph Zimmel

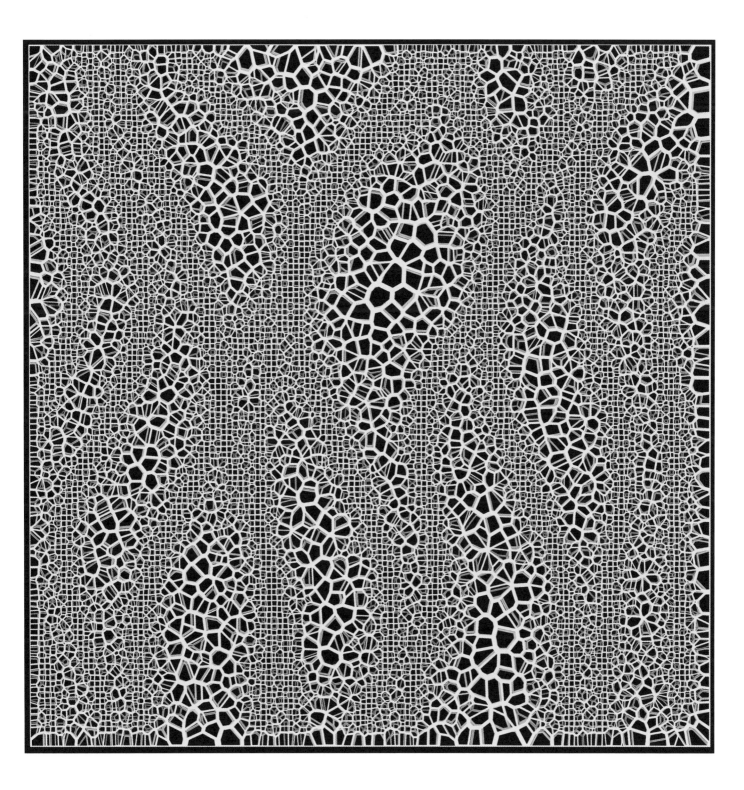

Porosity, Nicola Beck, Christoph Zimmel

STUDIO LYNN

Photo: Ari Marcopoulos

<u>Head</u>
Prof. Greg Lynn

<u>Assistant Professors</u>
Kristy Balliet
Oliver Bertram
Justin Diles

<u>Lecturers</u>
Martin Murero

<u>Organization</u>
Alexandra Graupner

Studio Greg Lynn focuses on the development of a new aesthetic that addresses the entire spectrum of architectural performance. This aesthetic shift from a modernist paradigm of identical, modular elements that emerged in the context of mechanization, toward compositions of varying, complexly linked individual elements.

The premise of this new aesthetic is the development of a new design sensibility, an expertise in rhythmic, soft forms and patterns that have been made possible through the use of computers and calculus-based geometry. In order to master these tools completely, the studio uses state-of-the-art computer and CNC technologies both in design and model fabrication.

This is done in reference not only to the professional work of Greg Lynn and his office Greg Lynn Form, but also in relation to progressive forces in architecture, design, art and other cultural fields.

Although or even because this work is an investigation into fields that are not yet completely known, the studio maintains an awareness of a greater cultural context. Design work is done in a dialogue between modernism and contemporary architectural precedents, as well as a continuous exchange with other disciplines like industrial design, fashion, music and film.

Theory

To ensure that a variety of ideas infuse the studio, theory meetings are periodically held to introduce and critically discuss relevant texts and current architectural questions. An internal studio theory reader accompanies the discussion.

Study trips

Instruction topics are supplemented by study trips, at least once per year. These experiences are intended to address both architecture and urbanism, but also a broader range of social and cultural concerns.

Hernan Diaz Alonso

THE RAIDER OF THE LOST TRUTH

Design Studios

The best way for architecture to be is to never be complete.

That said, maybe this is one of those issues that I don't pay much attention to or think about on a regular basis (part of my commitment to being less overtly intellectual) ...

... Except when, like here and now, I have to think about the work as if I was a detective observing an autopsy.

But, first, I would like to preface my remarks by saying that I understand the architect as a permanent seismographer of society and its culture and as such architecture can be constantly updated, revisited and modified. Permanence tells us less about architecture and more about societies that think they are permanent when they are not.

Studio Lynn, guided by his leader Greg, has been suffering my nonsense comments as a critic for the last 3 or 4 years, to be absolutely honest, I always thought that I get the better part of the deal, since it is one of the few places that I feel that I walk away knowing new things.

This has to do with the capacity of Greg Lynn, arguably the most influential figure in the discipline for the last fifteen years, to keep re-shaping his quest for the search of the "true architecture."

This, which sound like an obvious path for an educator, is very rare practice these days, in which cynicals and formulaic approaches to teaching have become the norm. The search for the truth is a much more complex condition, it requires a focus commitment and a deep knowledge of the discipline, it requires the constancy to always think in a critical way, but ultimately it requires a complete submersion in to the depth of the discipline's rigor. A practice that has been abandoned for most cases in the era of computational recourse in architecture.

For me, it has been an interesting transformation to see the evolution of Greg Lynn's method of thinking in relation to architecture and teaching at large, it seem to me that he started like Han Solo in the First Star Wars, as a very skillful pilot in control of his spaceship and destiny, but not much more beyond that area of enquire, then towards the "return of the Jedi", he is part of a much larger endeavor, but, just to keep with the Harrison Ford "Evolution" (my apologies to some European thinkers) it seems to me that Han Solo has morphed into Indiana Jones, and his shift towards the crusades in search for the truth and understanding of the trajectory and history of things.

Architecture can only exist in the present, and for that to occur it requires a deep understanding of its genealogy and its future, it requires a commitment to truth.

I cannot think of anybody or anywhere that this "thing" happens in a more committed way than that with Greg Lynn and his studio at the Angewandte ...

CRISIS : BANK

Winter term 2008/09

Banks pose a unique architectural question of transparency and security. There are two contemporary developments that make the problem of designing a bank interesting: the first is the use of electronic banking that makes trips to the bank and even a visit to the bank less critical; and the second is the collapse of multi-national banks due to the burst of the American and British real estate economy bubble.

The recent banking crisis has highlighted, among other things, the need for a revaluation of banking and its institutions. This semester we focused on private and boutique banking as a means to study an architecturally specific problem. The architectural and spatial design of a vault, with safety deposit boxes connotes security. The lobby, teller stations, desks, and even private offices of the bank connote transparency. At a less literal and more important institutional level the bank needs to express and atmospherically communicate both a secure space for valuable commodities as well as a transparent space of professionally supervised transactions in "the light of day." The secure vault and the transparent hall need consideration within the city. There are many ways to design the street, urban and/or exterior presence of the bank's interior on a façade and in addition to the sectional design of the bank in terms of security and transparency. The façade was a dominant design concern. The programmatic and functional aspects of the bank are very straightforward and it was the design of spatial enclosure and relationships regarding transparency, opacity, continuity, enclosure and façade that were of primary concern.

Bika Rebek

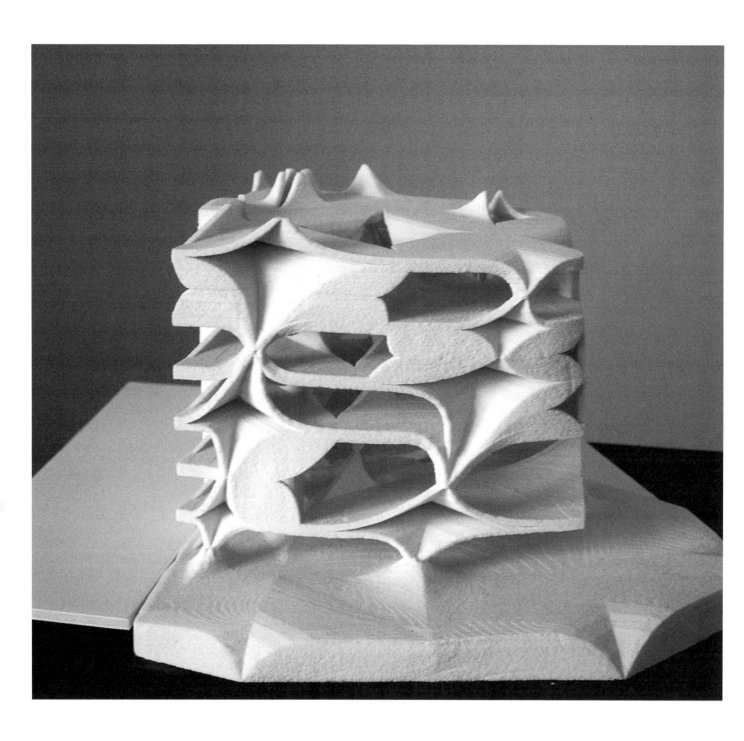

Anna Psenicka

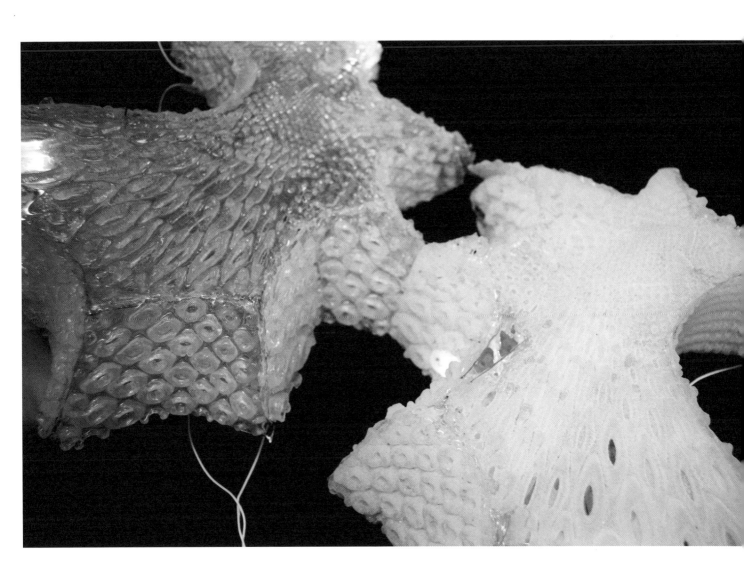

Bika Rebek

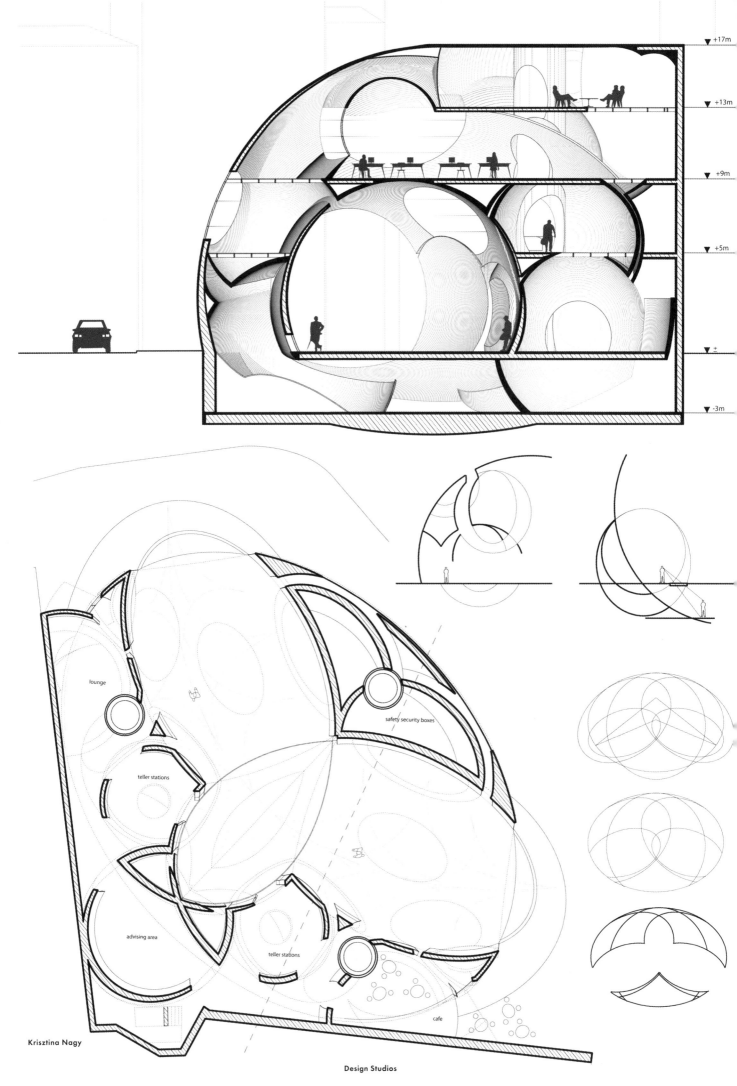

+17m

+13m

+9m

+5m

±

-3m

lounge

teller stations

advising area

teller stations

safety security boxes

cafe

Krisztina Nagy

Design Studios

96

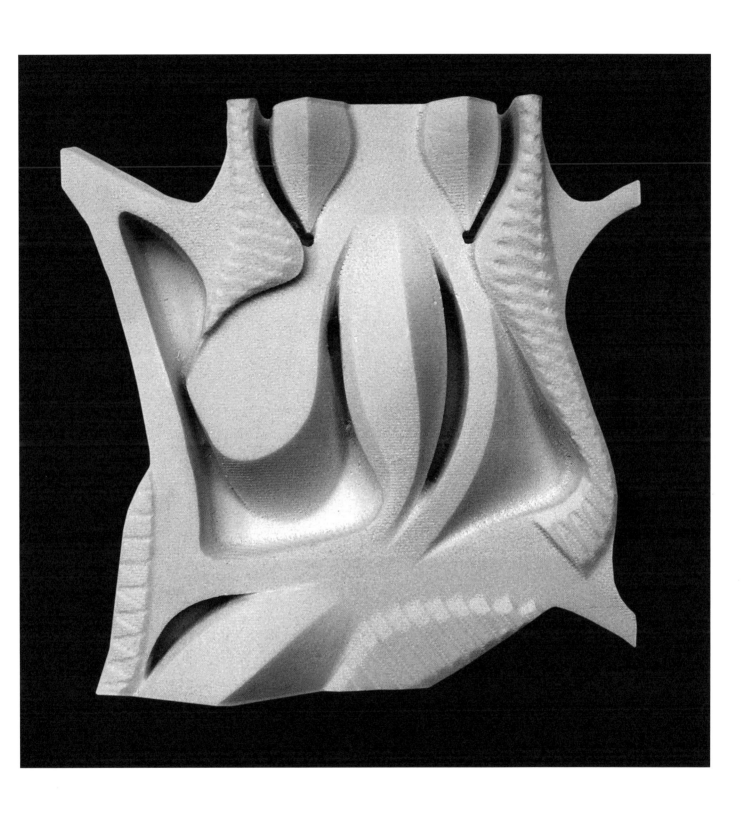

Curime Batliner, Jan Markus Ludwig

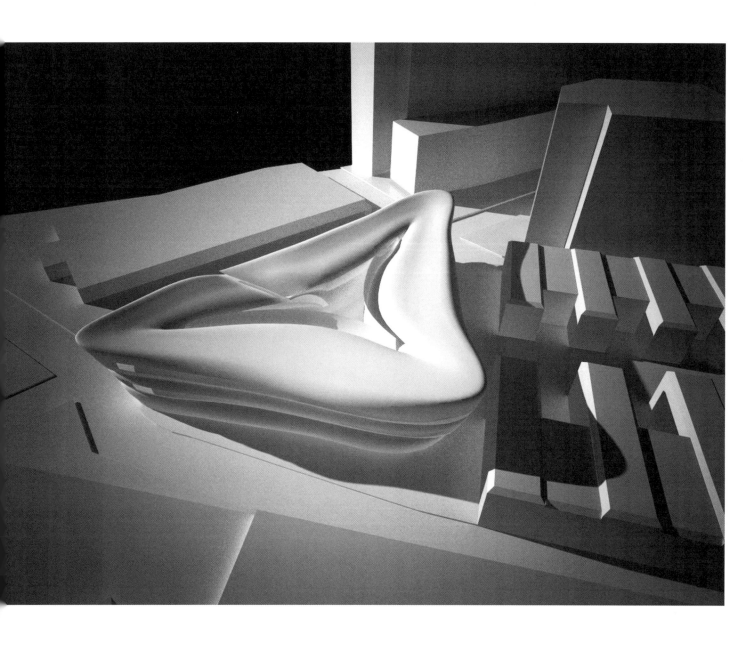

Melina Girardi, Emanuel Tornquist

Gregor Schindler

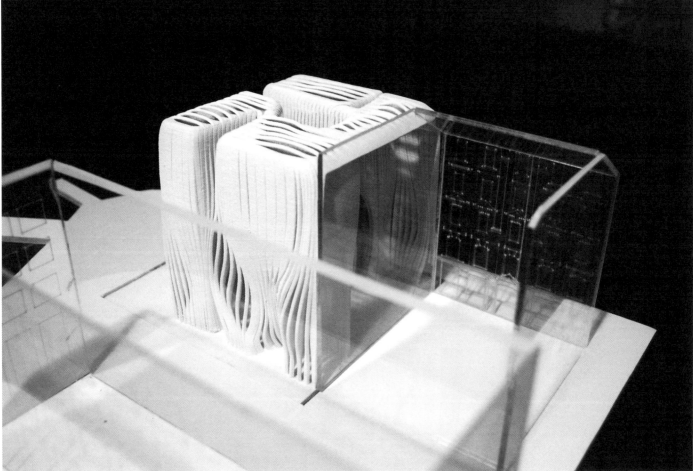

Miljan Radojevic

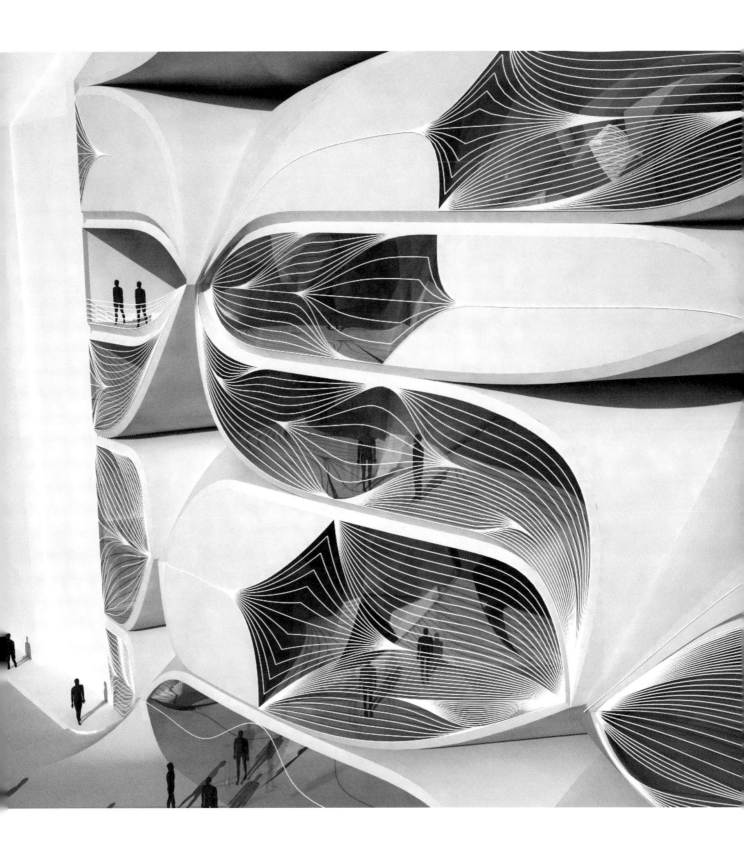

Anna Psenicka

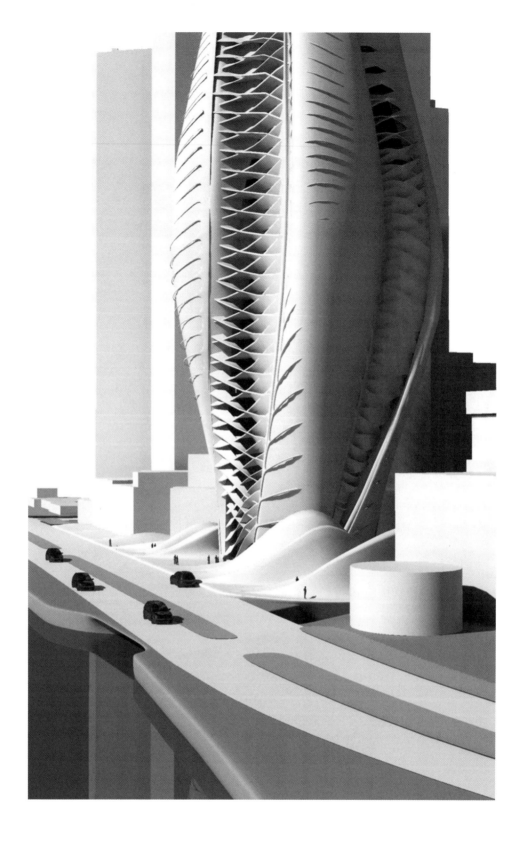

Julia Körner

Joanna Helinurm

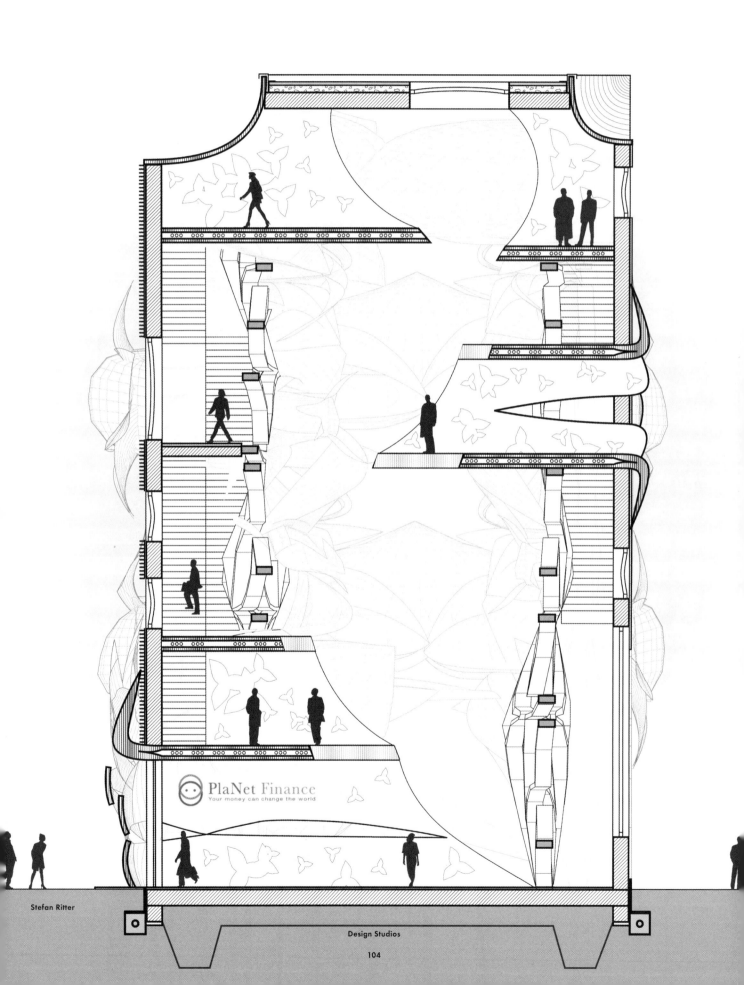

PlaNet Finance
Your money can change the world

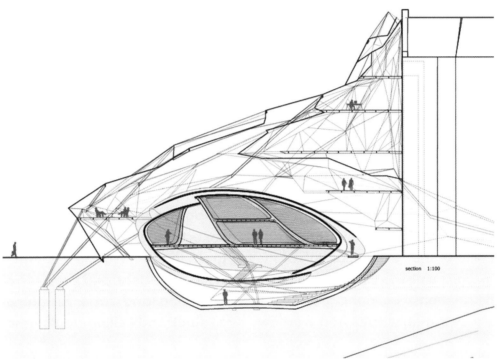

section 1:100

Verena Lihl

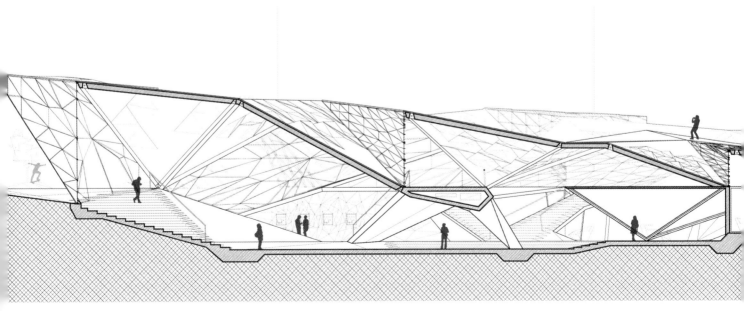

Susanna Ernst, Siim Tuksam

MASS AND LANDSCAPE

Summer term 2009

This term Studio Lynn developed an architecture of carving, hollowing, sculpting, thickness and poché. In a word, MASS. Mass is proposed as an alternative to another contemporary design strategy that transforms single surfaces into structural lattices, trellises or frames. To move away from the transformation of geometry into structural lineaments and towards mass and thickness, projects are conceptually monolithic and thought of as being carved from a single homogeneous material. Rather than employing a single surface and adding thickness later, students have paid careful attention to material depth by always designing with two surfaces. In these projects surfaces are not coincident or parallel but have variable mass between them to stress the difference between basic material thickness and designed poché. Designs are delineated as an assembly of elements through coursing, bonding and other masonry-like articulations of masses that are stacked, poured, carved or formed.

The relationship between architectural mass and natural landscape was also a topic this term. Students visited homes and gardens designed by the early 20th century architect Edwin Lutyens before working in teams to develop a small campus for a boarding school in the English countryside. Designs proceed from discrete, formal architectural elements rather than from the "planning" of the site or the "organization" of the program into adjacencies, clumps, clusters or shapes. Each project embeds its core spatial concepts in very clear and concise volumes with distinct and subtle relationships to the ground and surrounding landscape. Functional qualities are derived from views, adjacencies and windows; wall, floor and ceiling depth; and enclosure in general.

The project site has several important distant view elements: scenic ponds and a village-like housing development. Projects carefully craft the relationship of foreground landscapes and buildings and middle distance outdoor rooms and buildings to these background elements. Walls, mounds, plantings, buildings and the ground itself are used to obscure, frame and hide middle distance and distant views. The designs function like the picturesque buildings and gardens the students visited, where landscapes work spatially through vignettes (perspectives) that are linked one to another by vistas and modulated by the ground topology, plantings and building masses.

Siim Tuksam, Melina Girardi, Lisa Sommerhuber

Emanuel Tornquist, Karl Breinesberger, Barna Kovacs

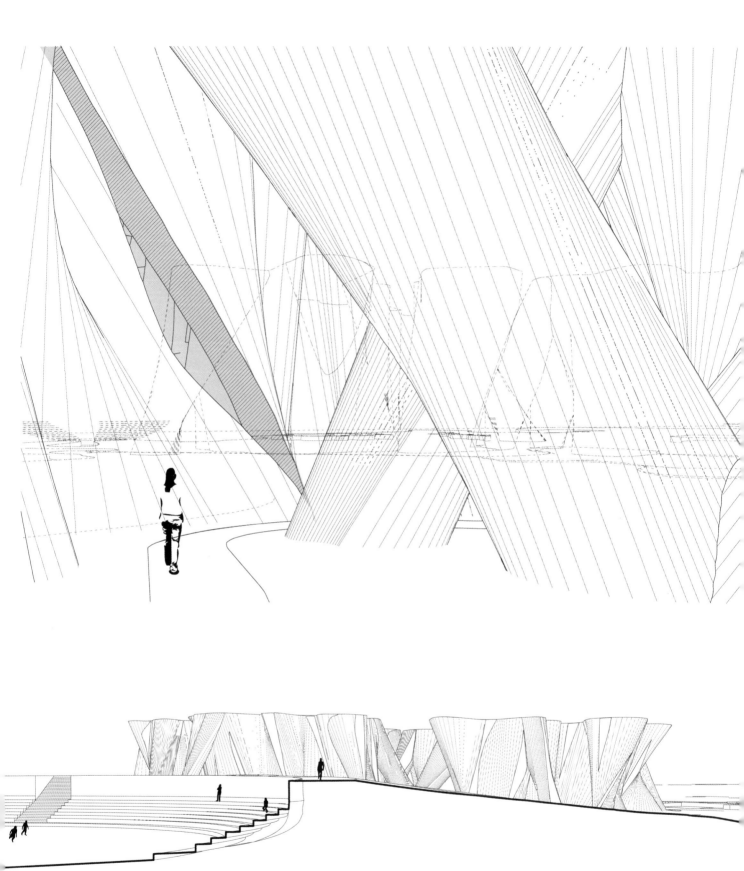

Mirko Daneluzzo, Florian Fend, Joanna Helinurm

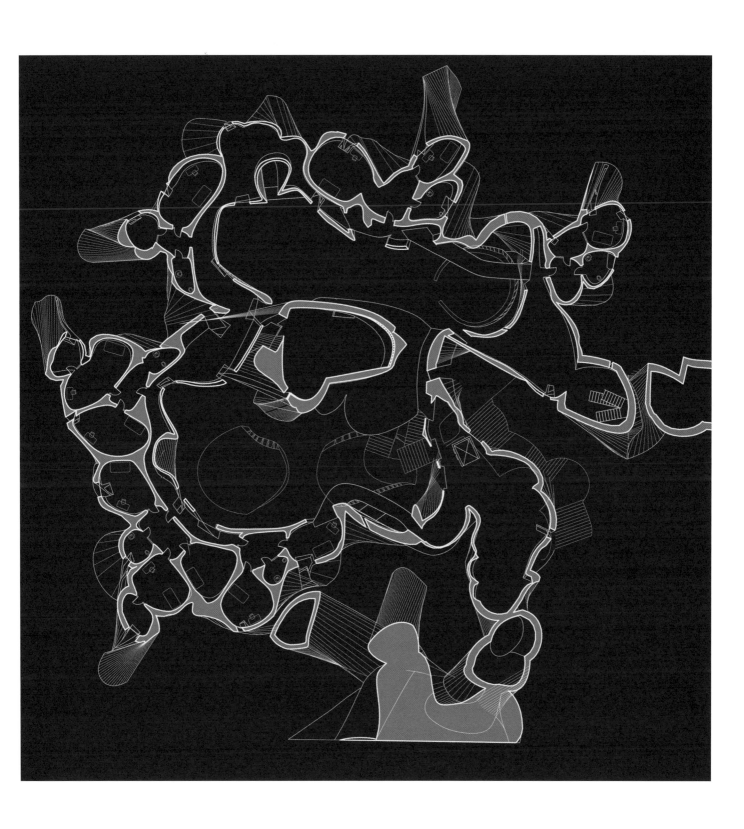

Mirko Daneluzzo, Florian Fend, Joanna Helinurm

Miljan Radojevic, Martina Lesjak, Ines Klausberger

1. Mass

2. Mass + Inner Space

3. Inner Space + Programm Stamp

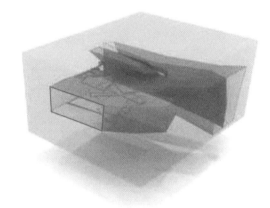

4. Inner Space + Programm Stamp + Apertures

5. Shape

6. Shape + Stamp from Outside

7. Shape + Stamp from Outside + Landscape

8. Result

Jan Markus Ludwig, Baptiste Bernard, Ioana Petkova

Bika Rebek, Krisztina Nagy, Susanna Ernst

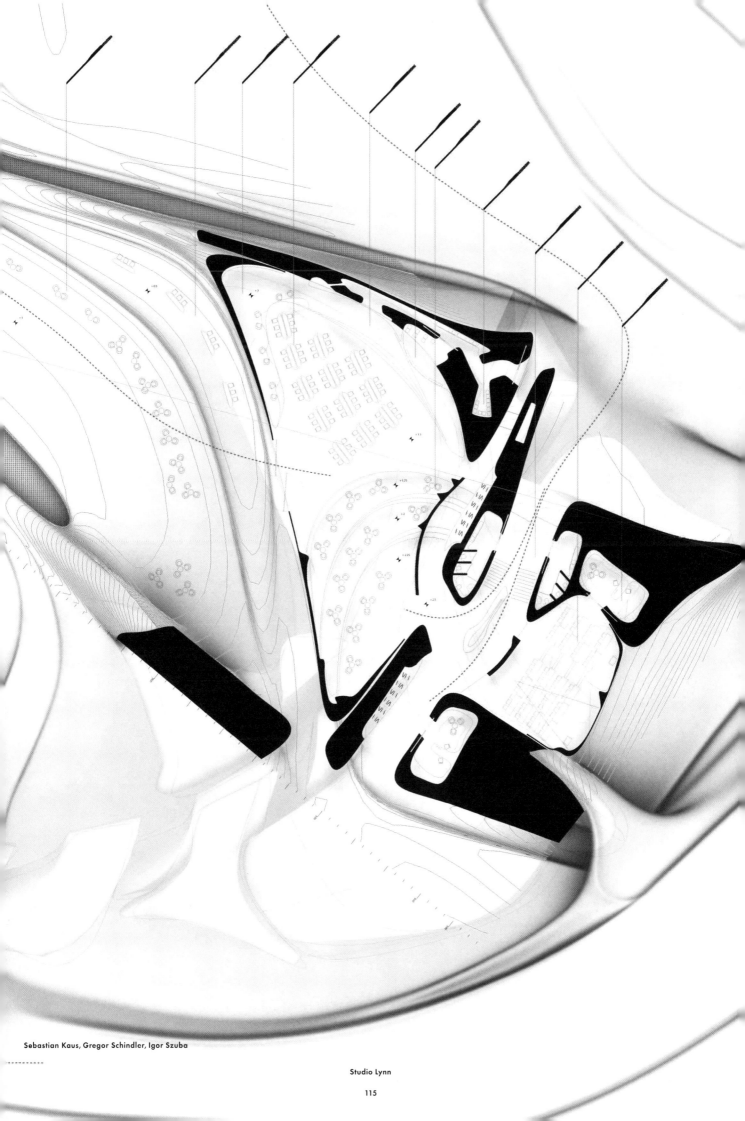

Sebastian Kaus, Gregor Schindler, Igor Szuba

STUDIO PRIX

Photo: Manfred Klimek

<u>Head</u>
Prof. Wolf D. Prix

<u>Assistant Professors</u>
Anja Jonkhans
Niels Jonkhans
Reiner Zettl

<u>Lecturers</u>
Sophie Grell
Armin Hess
Bärbel Müller
Franz Sam

<u>Workshop/Videolab</u>
Peter Strasser

<u>Organization</u>
Angelika Zelisko

The future of our profession can be gleaned from the screens and models of our students. These theoretical buildings are still free of economic and political constraints and the emergent concepts have not yet been eroded by reality.

Our studio has more resemblance with a creative lab that offers intense support. Here the students are able to learn to develop strategies and to design spaces based on designed shapes and tangible models and to structure them analytically in ground plan and section.

We use the dialectic between understanding and grasping as feedback between model and computer, thus expanding the repertory of our design tools.

Urban planning concepts are addressed just as buildings as public spaces since the reinterpretation of public space is an important theme of this studio.

By studying social references of architecture as well as the application of construction principles as a form-defining element, we are able to define new aesthetic concepts. Here the goal is to transcend traditional boundaries.

The international review guests in our studio share important information on the works of other schools which can serve as a basis of comparison. Workshops and exhibitions in Austria and other countries also serve as a platform for discussion and thus for the exchange of ideas. Excursions to the important buildings of architectural history take us to Moscow, London, France, Italy, Germany, Switzerland, Croatia and Portugal. Special projects such as *Techo in Mexico*, a workshop in Oaxaca, Mexico where seven students constructed a roof as an emblem for a new cultural center are based on the notion that information can only become knowledge through experience.

Eric Owen Moss

WHAT'S A PRIX STUDIO?

Design Studios

"We sit here stranded,
*though we're all doing our best to deny it…."**

What's a Prix Studio?

Listen for what you don't hear.
Look for what you don't see.

Dramatis persona: Architecture, the introvert.
Belongs to itself alone.
Dramatis persona: Architecture, the extrovert.
Mandates the world around it.
How?
That's a Prix Studio.

"You shouldn't take it so personal."

Architecture moves.
Better?
Worse?
Different.
The movers?
That's a Prix Studio.

"I ask him what the matter was, but I know
that he don't talk."

Revolutionary today.
Staid tomorrow.
No language.
No rule.
No system,
No method.
Undo.
Overdue.
Why?
That's a Prix Studio.

"Louise holds a handful of rain telling you
to defy it."

To see and to see.
To see and to understand.
To see what you don't see.
So?
That's a Prix Studio.

Durable's
incurable.

Theories neglect.
Hypotheses omit.
Whole's not whole.

Interrogate whole's whole.
Architecture gets different.
Where?
A Prix Studio.

"Mona Lisa must 'ave had the highway blues.
You can tell by the way she smiles."

The box.
Unboxed.
The erstwhile foe.
Enfeebled.
Outside the box?
A new rule.
Inside the box?
An old method.
Architecture needs an adversary.
Who is it?
A Prix Studio.

"The ghost of electricity howls in the bones
of her face."

Architecture and surprise.
Surprise and experiment.
If surprise is no surprise,
Experiment's no experiment.
And architecture ain't architecture.

"He brags of his misery. He likes to live
dangerously."

Architecture: the most precise exegesis of
the principles that make it what it is.
How to construct it?

Dramatis persona: Overt architecture.
You get is what you see.
Dramatis persona: Covert architecture.
You get what you don't see.

"Inside the museum infinity goes up on trial."

Should it fly?
Architecture, the analogue model:
Moons, clouds, monsters.
Architecture, the algorithmic model:
The computer's chronology.
Where?
A Prix Studio.

Eric Owen Moss, Los Angeles, June 2010

* Quotations with apologies to Bob Dylan

Studio project

EXTREMES

Winter term 2008/9

The studio topic deals with the notion of building in extreme environments.

The functional focus of the buildings develops gradually from a small research station – as a single highly specialized living/working unit – to a hotel – as an agglomeration of highly specialized units.

The technical focus lies on adaptable and responsive structures that react to external forces. Aspects of energetic sustainability in connection with functional performance will drive the adaption to – or the deformation by – external influences.

Students research and define locations for small-scale research stations.

Where can be researched what, why, by whom and for how long?

The result will lead to a simple performance brief for the research pods.

Students design a performative shell. Transformability and adaptability are the key requirements. Adaptability of structure allows for different performances. The minimum of three different states will be explored and demonstrated. How does the research station deals with dynamic external forces (avoidance or absorption)?

Its development is driven by the iterative work with physical models (experiment and representation) and digital drawings. Brian Cody, Klaus Bollinger and teams provide specialist tutoring.

Stefanie Theuretzbacher

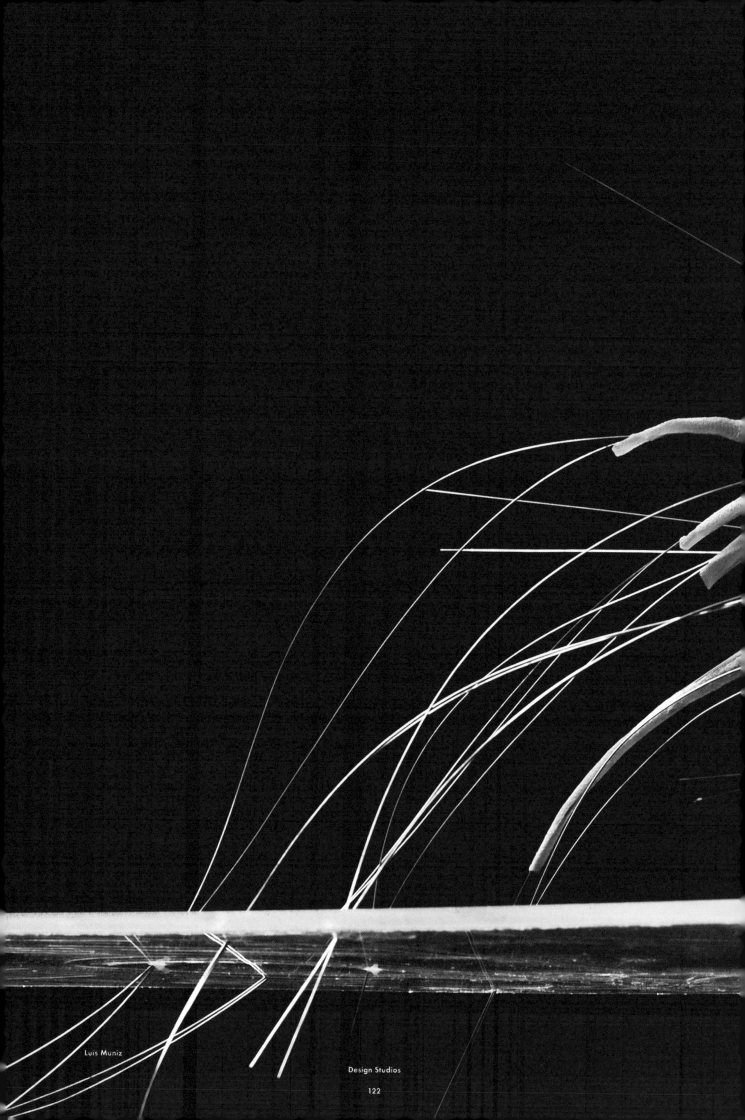

Luis Muniz

Design Studios

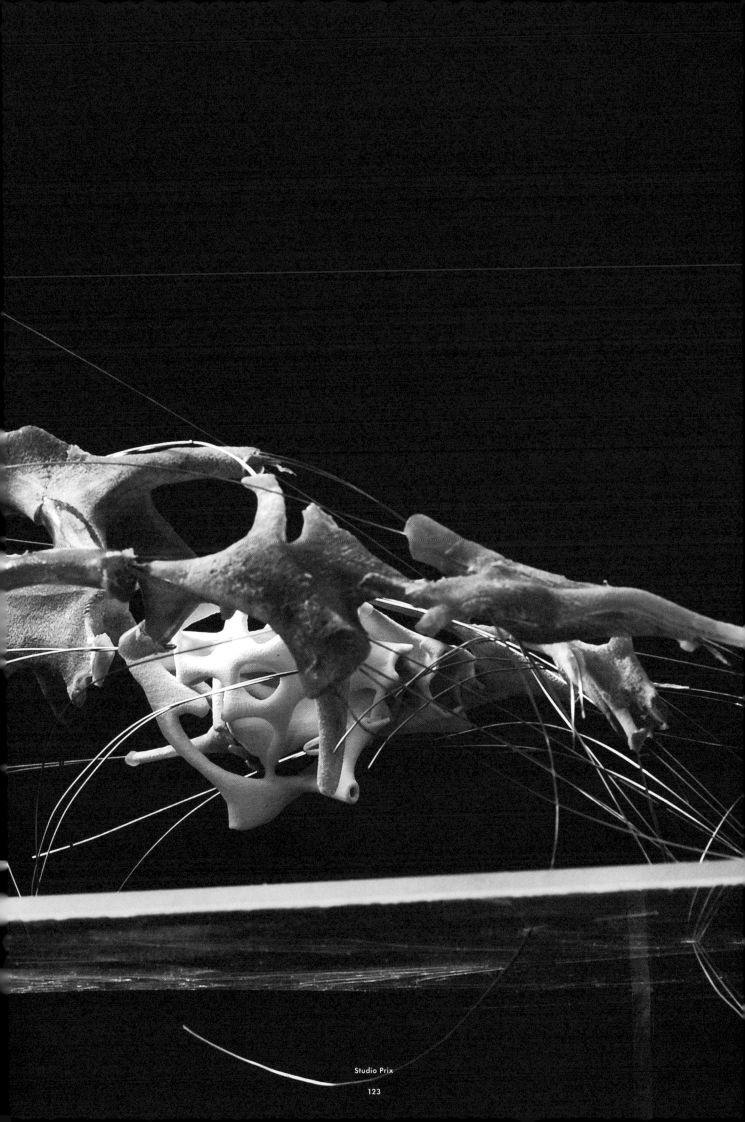

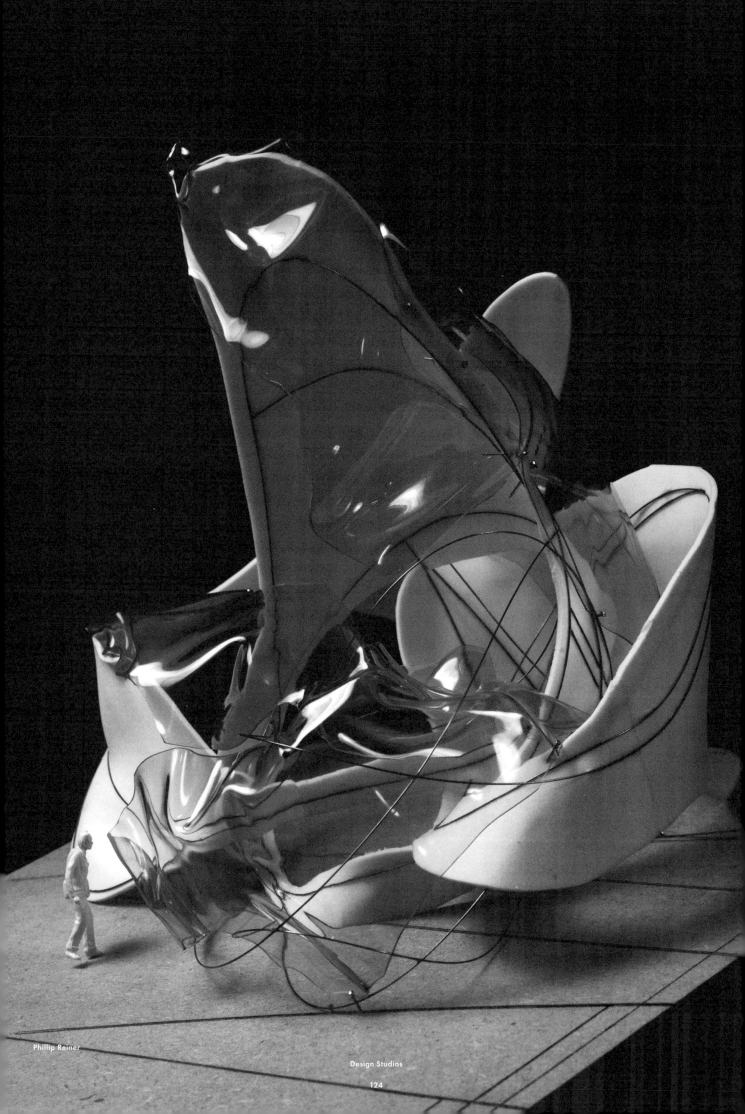

Phillip Reiner

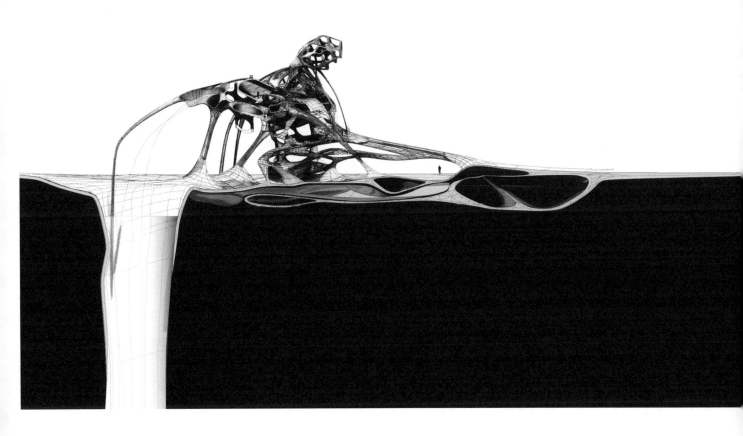

Luis Muniz

Lukas Allner

Studio Prix

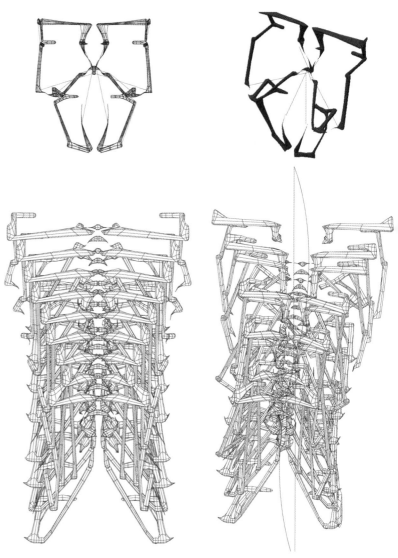

Yichen Lu

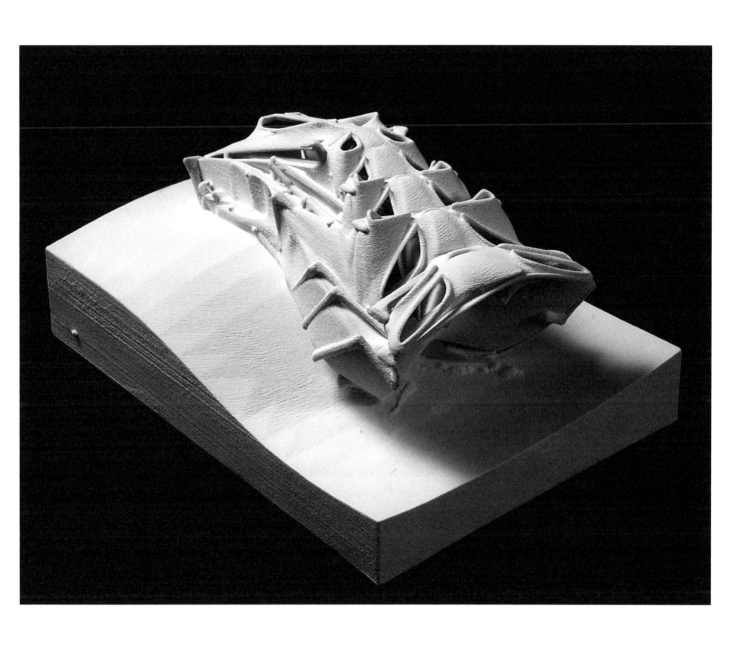

Yichen Lu

POWER RISE

Summer term 2009

The program aims to design a high-rise in Vienna that is able to transform energy through exposure to contextual dynamic forces (wind, solar).

The focus is placed on the overall geometry according to the energy concept and on the development of the building skin. The function of the building is a classic (big) inner city program of retail in the base of the tower, office spaces and a hotel with amenities located centrally and residential areas in the upper section of the tower. Underground car parking for 1000 cars with access to the public streets needs to be provided.

It is obligatory to consult specialists in the fields of energy design and structure during the entire development.

Chronology

Part I (research): The semester starts with the analysis of given examples of fluid dynamics. Students simulate effects and phenomena through the use of digital simulation tools. The aim is to explore the effect that dynamic movement has on non-dynamic forms (distortion, abrasion, compression etc.)

Part II (model studies): Students examined technologies that are suitable to transform dynamic movement into energy (heat, electricity) and sketched concepts of their own proposal for a façade element that would use these principles.

Part III (building): Based on the research of dynamic forces and the subsequent model studies, both virtual and physical, students are given the high-rise brief.

Focus is placed on process: the development using various digital tools for evaluating the performance of the building as well as the customary procedures of using model making and drafting.

Computer simulations of certain phenomena of fluid dynamics are made to demonstrate the dynamic behavior of liquids of various viscosities.

The students are looking into the behavior of turbulent and laminar flow of liquid and air (particles) along surfaces and objects. Effects of abrasion, debris, deformation and compression are analyzed using analytic simulation software.

Apart from getting accustomed to a new set of tools the students learn about concepts and definitions of basic fluid dynamics and quantitative relations important for the assessment of cause-and-effect for the subsequent development of dynamic performative buildings.

Results of analytical software tools inform the development of physical models. The process of feedback between drawing techniques, both 2D and 3D, evaluation of performance through analysis (software) and the construction of physical scale models are the backbone of the design process in the studio.

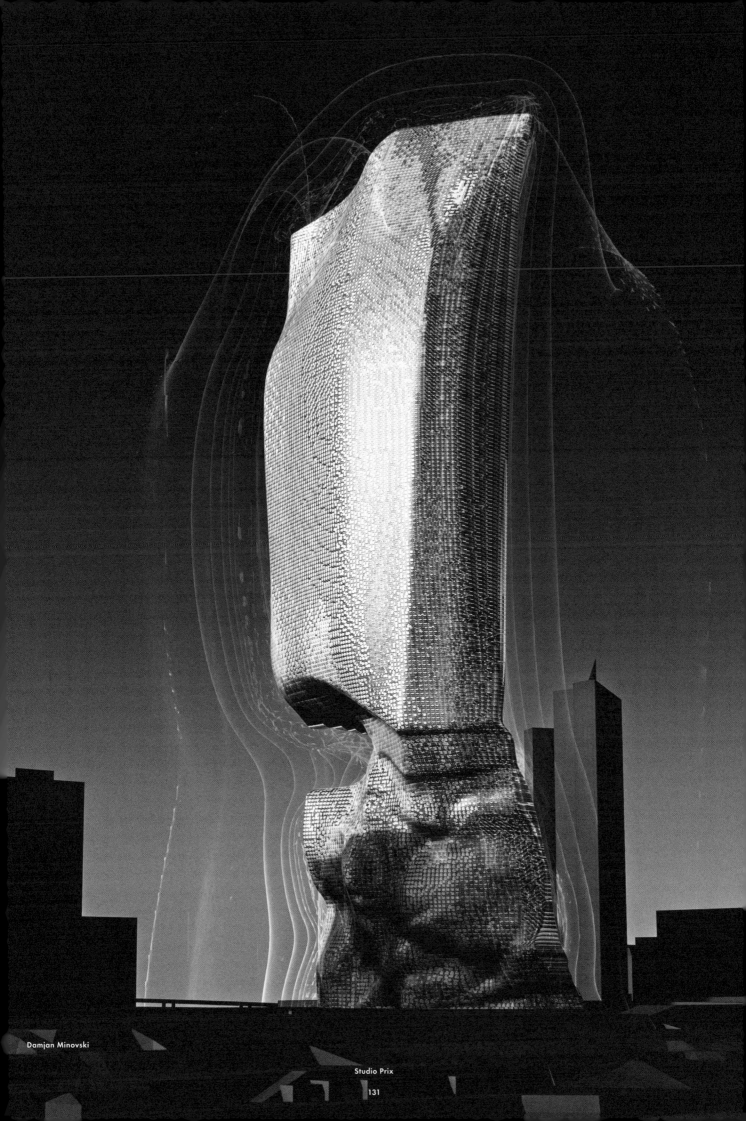

Damjan Minovski

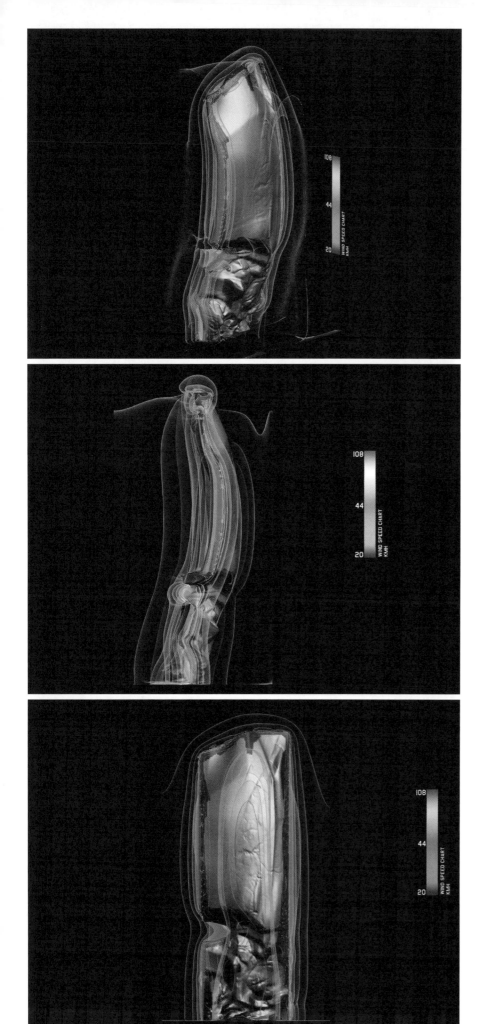

Damjan Minovski

Damjan Minovski

Daniela Kröhnert

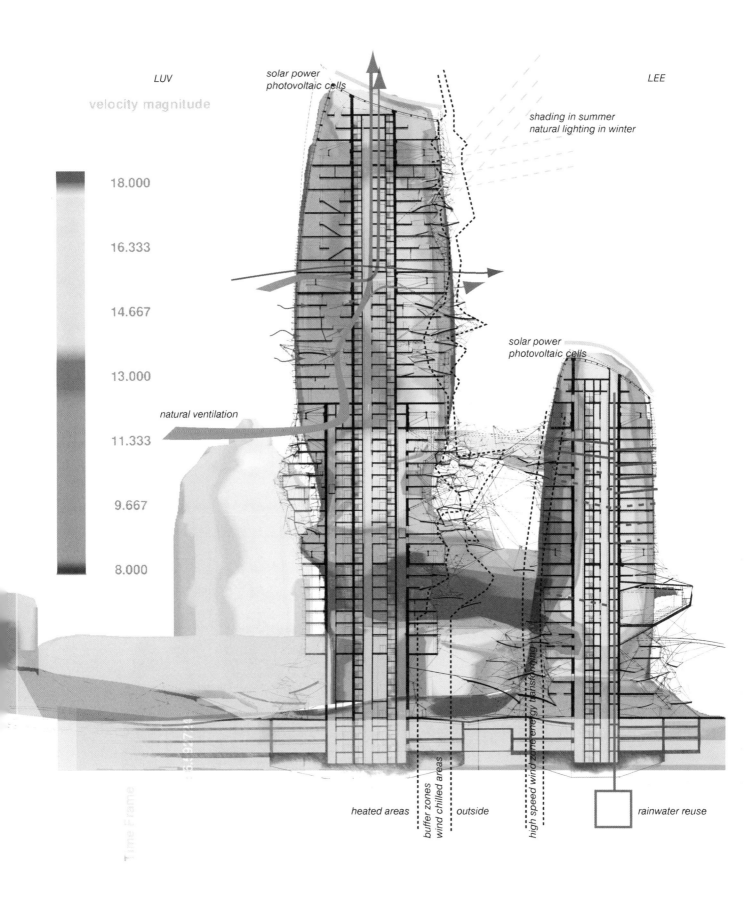

LUV

velocity magnitude

solar power
photovoltaic cells

LEE

shading in summer
natural lighting in winter

18.000

16.333

14.667

13.000

solar power
photovoltaic cells

natural ventilation

11.333

9.667

8.000

heated areas

buffer zones
wind chilled areas

outside

high speed wind zone energy transforming

rainwater reuse

Daniela Kröhnert

ENERGY SURFACE – ANALYSIS

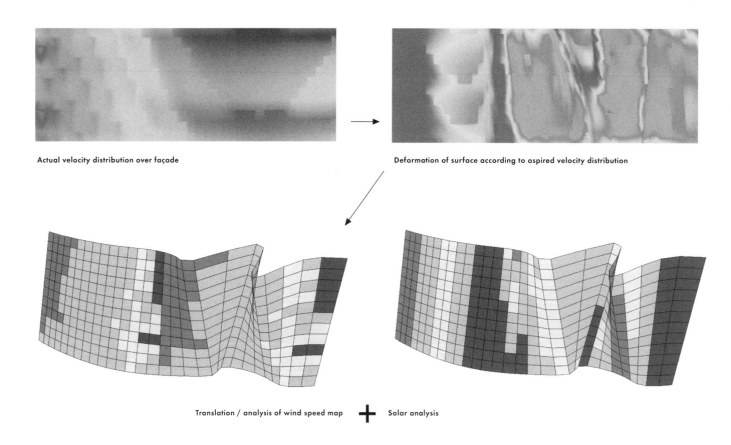

Actual velocity distribution over façade

Deformation of surface according to aspired velocity distribution

Translation / analysis of wind speed map **+** Solar analysis

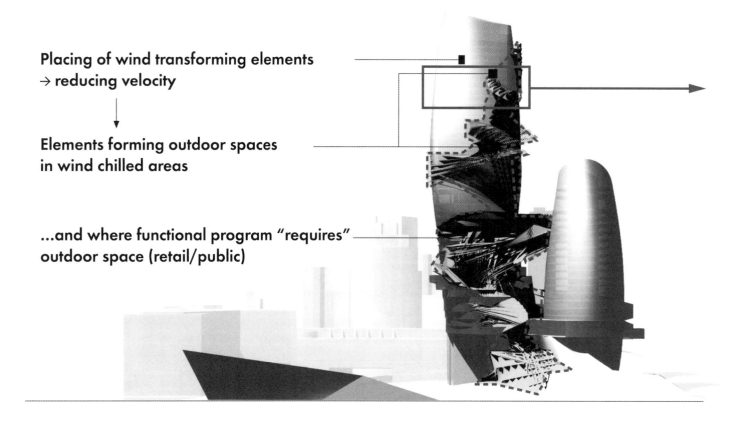

Placing of wind transforming elements
→ reducing velocity

Elements forming outdoor spaces
in wind chilled areas

...and where functional program "requires"
outdoor space (retail/public)

Daniela Kröhnert

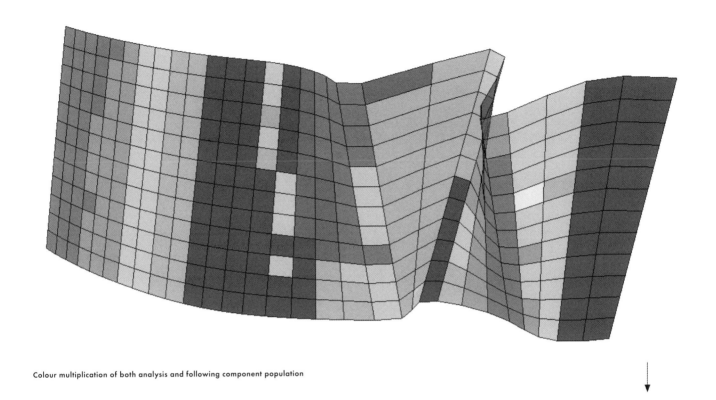

Colour multiplication of both analysis and following component population

Energy transformers

Wind breakers

"Balcomnies"

Fixed points

Façade

Flexible points

Rods

Initial state of surface

Magnet

Inductors

Planar surfaces

HP surfaces

Warped surfaces by data mapping

Studio Prix

Dominik Strzelec

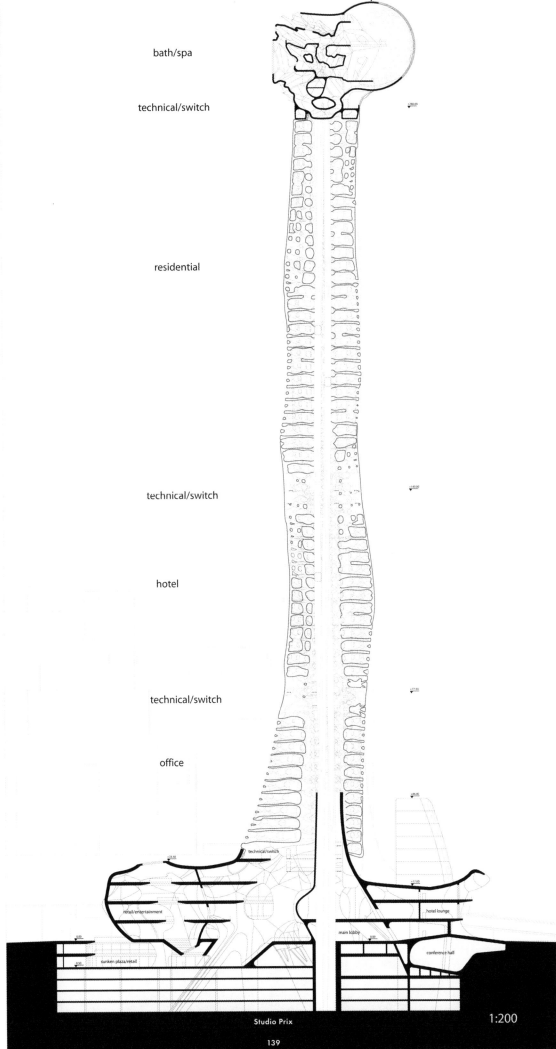

bath/spa

technical/switch

residential

technical/switch

hotel

technical/switch

office

technical/switch

retail/entertainment

sunken plaza/retail

hotel lounge

main lobby

conference hall

Dominik Strzelec

Studio Prix

139

1:200

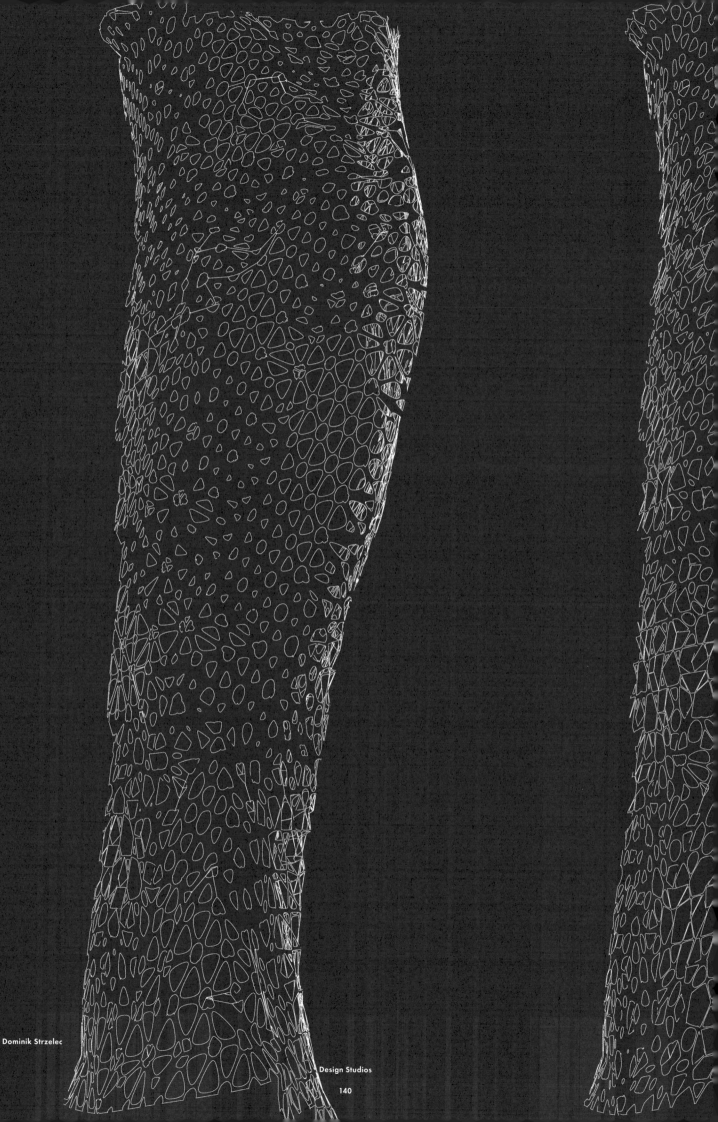

Dominik Strzelec

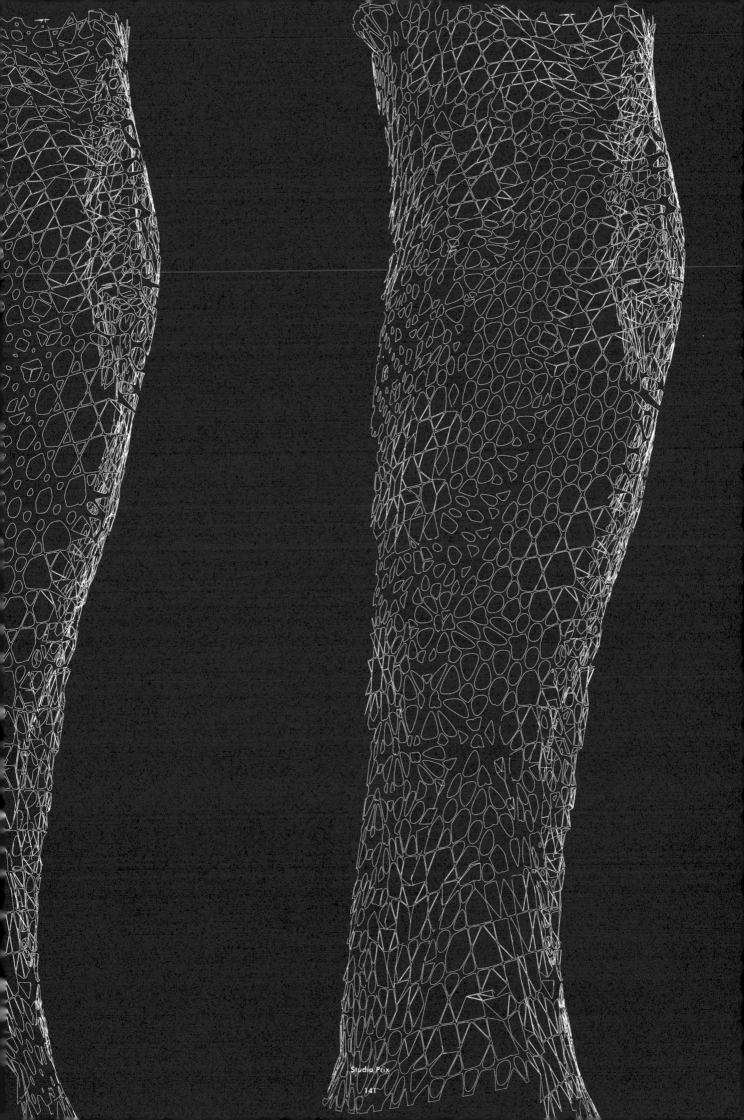

Oliver Lösser

Moritz Heimrath

CROSS OVER STUDIO

(N)CERTAINTIES

Head
François Roche

Tutors
Marc Fornes
Stephan Henrich
Manfred Hermann

Students
Mirta Bilos
Mirko Daneluzzo
Jan Gronkiewicz
Vladimir Ivanov
Martin Kleindienst
Martina Lesjak
Valerie Messini
Galo Moncayo
Rasa Navasaityte
Adam Orlinski
Raffael Petrovic
Dominik Strzelec

(n)certainties

In power games (apparatuses could be considered) relationship strategies supporting types of knowledge and supported by themselves.
—Michel Foucault, *Dits et Ecrits*

Machines are always pretending to do more than what they were programmed to do. It's their nature.

Their behavior alternates phantasms, frustrations and fears inspired by their own ability to break free and threaten us.

The blurriness between what they are supposed to do, as perfect alienated and domesticated creatures, and the anthropomorphic psychology we intentionally project onto them, creates a spectrum of potentiality, both interpretative and productive, which is able to re-"scenarize" the operating processes of the architectural field. Machines are vectors of narration, generators of rumor, and at the same time directly operational, with an accurate efficiency of production.

These multiple disorders, this kind of schizophrenia, could be considered a tool for reopening processes and subjectivities, for re-"protocolizing" indeterminacy and uncertainties. In this way, they become agents of fuzzy logic, of reactive and re-programmable logic.

As in *Alice in Wonderland*, where Lewis Carroll used mathematics to confuse a little girl's perception, such apparatuses, including "bachelor machines",[1] stretch a line of subjectivization to organize repetitions and anomalies[2] using and developing paradoxes that are able to re-complexify and de-alienate the edges of the truth system, in order to re-invert the logic of meaning and turn it into a vanishing point.

Their skyzoïd-machinism agendas are both products and vectors of paranoia.[3]

---

1 In the sense of Marcel Duchamp and Picabia.
2 In the sense of Difference and Repetition, G. Deleuze, 1968.
3 In both senses, "critical paranoia" and "pathological paranoia".

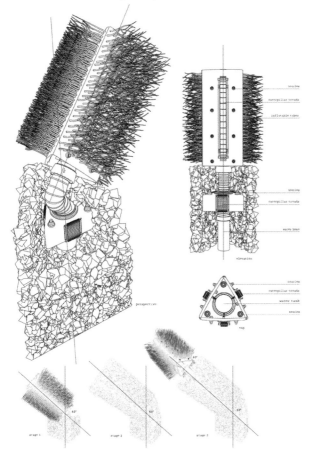

Raffael Petrovic

Adam Orlinsky

Raffael Petrovic

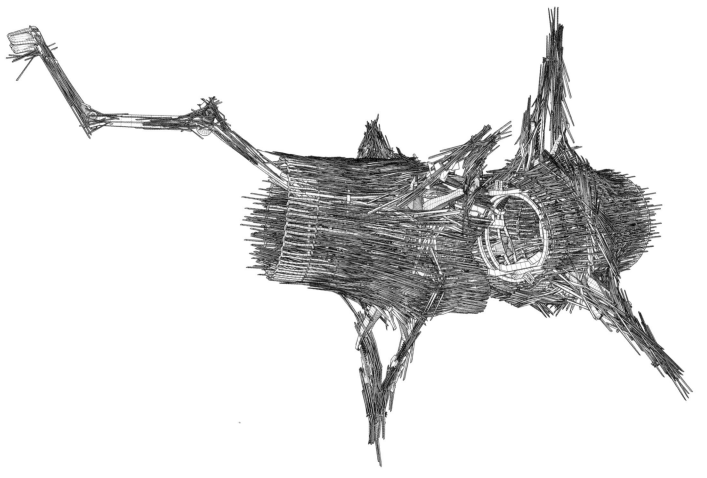

Adam Orlinsky

Cross Over Studio

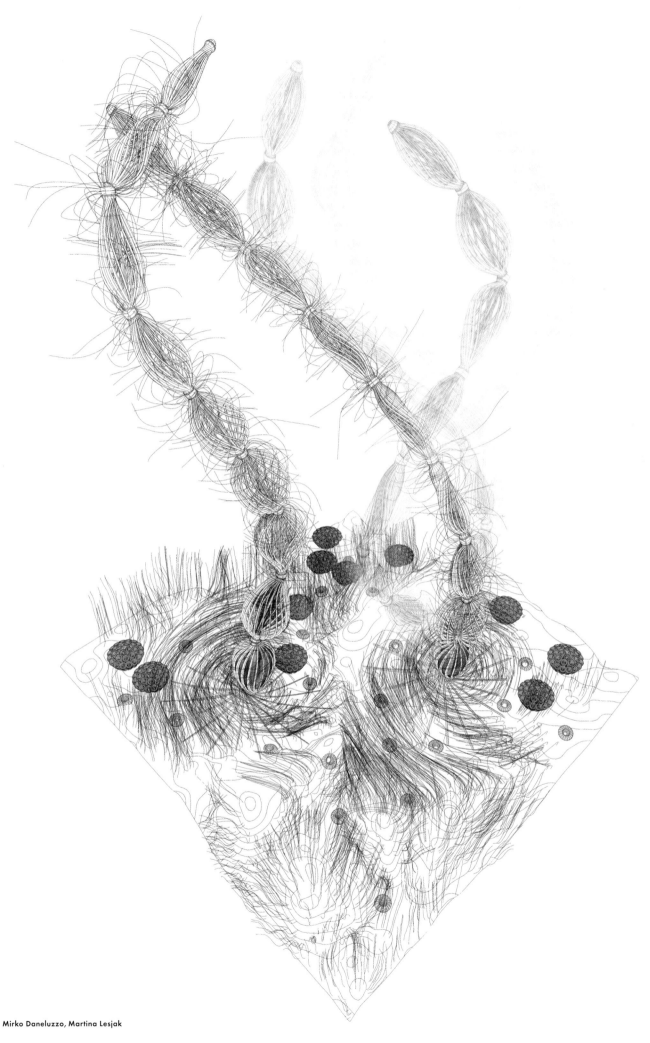

Mirko Daneluzzo, Martina Lesjak

STRUC-
TURAL
DESIGN

Head
Prof. Klaus Bollinger

Assistant Professor
Wilfried Braumüller

Lecturers
Arne Hofmann
Florian Medicus
Clemens Preisinger
Wolfgang Winter

The state of the art in designing engineering structures depends to a large degree on procedures and assumptions that date back to the 19th century. That time saw the advent of a new construction material with considerable tensile strength, namely steel. In the wake of and in combination with this innovation new statical calculation methods gave rise to buildings of hitherto unknown height or free span. These calculation procedures rest on a categorization of statical systems that still influences present day thinking. More or less all effective load bearing structures exhibit a high degree of regularity. They usually have one or more axes of symmetry. Some utilize arch or catenary shapes, but most consist of a large number of similar or identical elements. The structure's geometry was and is heavily influenced by what engineers are able to handle and thus to calculate efficiently.

Three recent developments in the field of civil engineering will help to overcome the above-mentioned limits:

First: advances in soft- and hardware make it possible to easily and swiftly assess a structure's statical properties.

Second: State-of-the-art optimization procedures that are partly inspired by nature allow one to search large solution spaces in reasonable amounts of time.

Third: computer-aided fabrication methods facilitate the economic production of customized structural components.

These three developments can be combined to generate structures with intrinsic load-bearing mechanisms. Their design contradicts the traditional conception of an engineering approach which consists of an a priori selection of the main structural components according to external boundary conditions. Instead the statical system ermerges from the design process according to intrinsic principles of the optimization algorithm and the given boundary conditions.

There is a high density of individuals in the vicinity of the best solution so far. Given enough computational resources the globally best solution will eventually emerge from the optimization process.

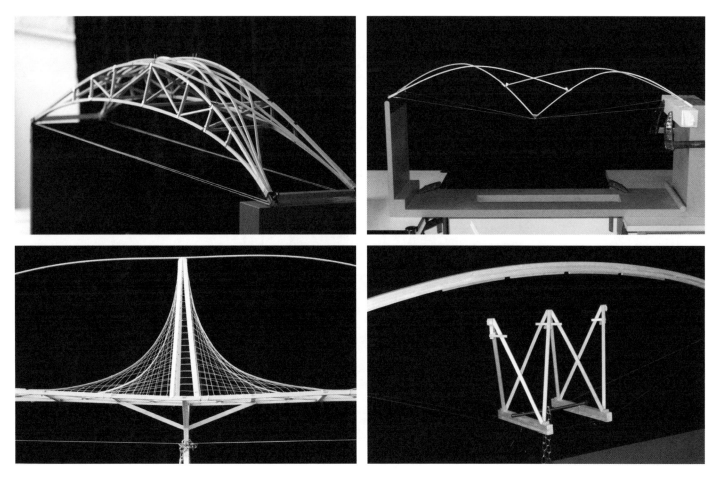

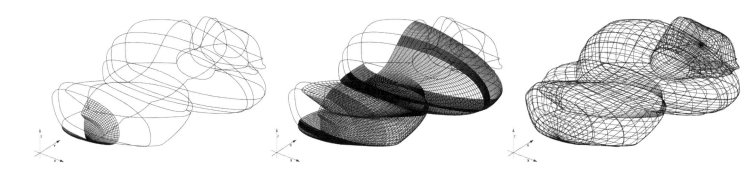

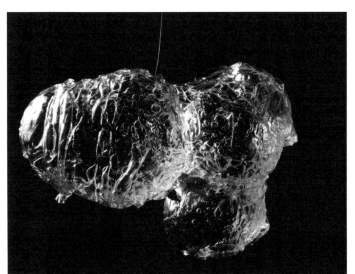

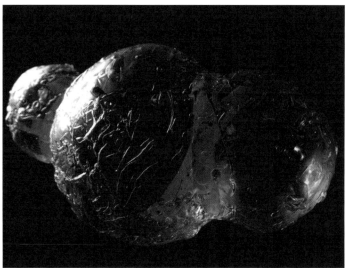

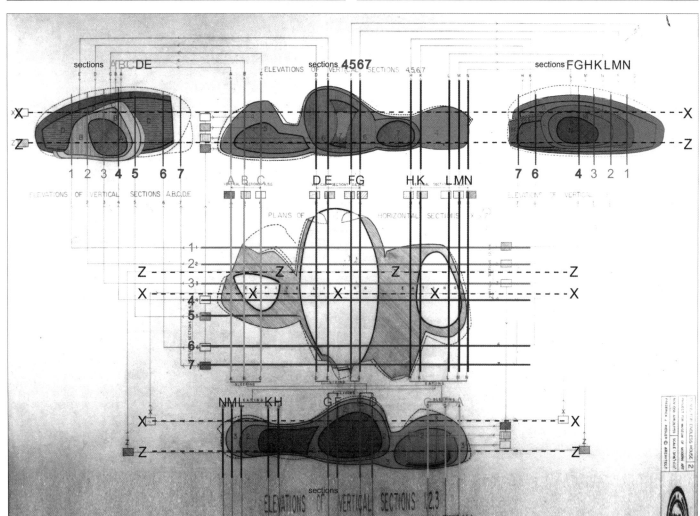

Seminar: *Friedrich Kiesler – Inside the Endless House*

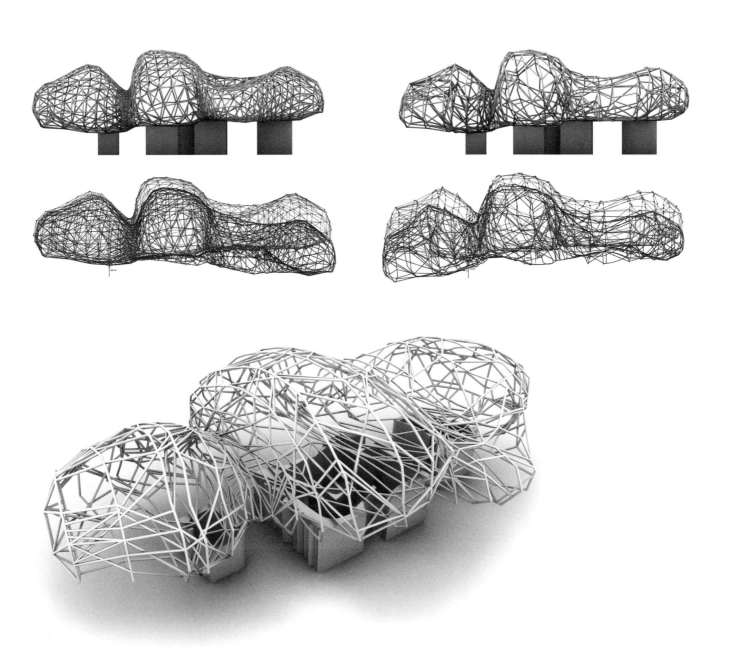

Structural Design

ENERGY
DESIGN

Head
Prof. Brian Cody

Assistant Professor
Bernhard Sommer

At Energy Design we pursue the goal in teaching and research of maximizing the energy performance of buildings by optimizing the form and construction.

Substantial main points of research are investigations regarding the relationship between building form and energy efficiency. The early employment of technology during the system design in terms of computer simulation can mean e.g. the prevention of technology such as air conditioning systems in the ready-made building.

By an interdisciplinary approach in the very beginning of the design process, the success of energy-efficient design shall be ensured. The field should not be left to a few specialists who often enough create architecture of poor design. On the contrary, energy efficient design must be combined with the most daring architecture. Only architects, who are free of prejudice and who employ the most cutting-edge techniques for their design process, will bring it to its full potential.

Research and teaching thus investigates Rapid Manufacturing, Interactive Architecture, Form and Energy Consumption, Parametric Design Strategies, all of which aim at the creation of Zero-Energy Buildings.

ADAPTABILITY RESEARCH

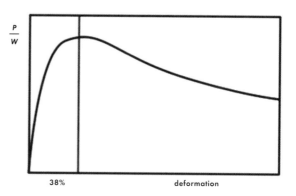

Figure 1: Inflation pressure P and strain energy density W against inflation ratio: for a spherical skin

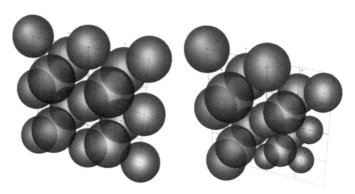

Figure 2: A cluster of space filling knots and their behavior

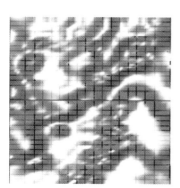

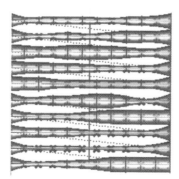

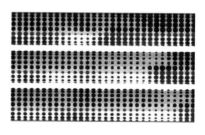

Figure 3: Translation of a graphic pattern into the deflation behavior of a row of tubes. The fringes stay rigid.
On the right: distribution of the rigid material in the hyper-elastic skin of three tubes

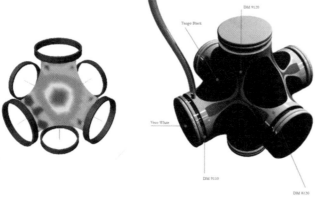

Figure 4: Curvature analysis, accordingly knot design and printed knot

Bernhard Sommer, Norbert Palz

Energy Design

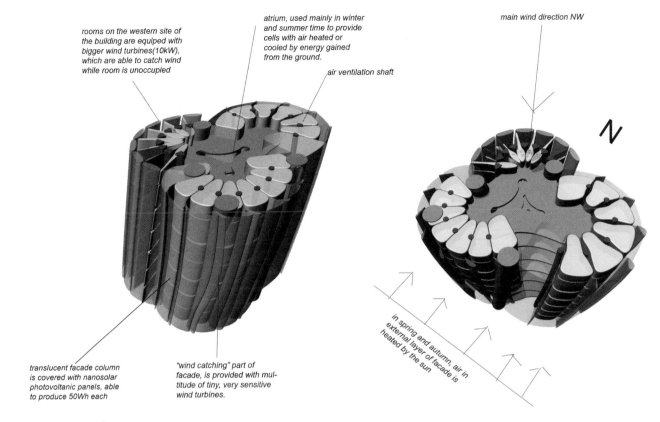

rooms on the western site of the building are equiped with bigger wind turbines(10kW), which are able to catch wind while room is unoccupied

atrium, used mainly in winter and summer time to provide cells with air heated or cooled by energy gained from the ground.

air ventilation shaft

main wind direction NW

N

translucent facade column is covered with nanosolar photovoltanic panels, able to produce 50Wh each

"wind catching" part of facade, is provided with multitude of tiny, very sensitive wind turbines.

in spring and autumn, air in external layer of facade is heated by the sun

Energy Design Concept, Jan Gronkiewicz

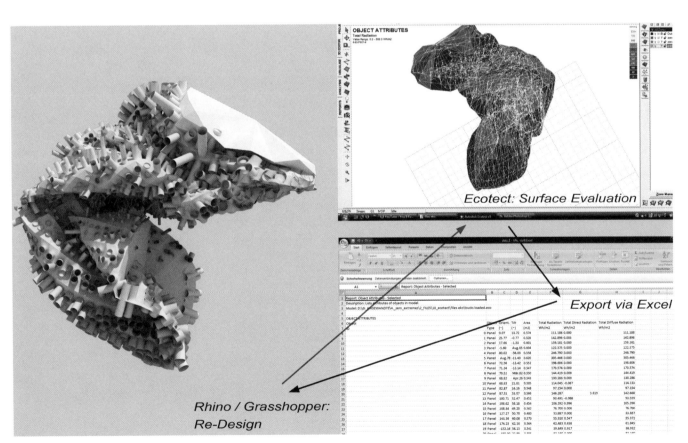

Ecotect: Surface Evaluation

Export via Excel

Rhino / Grasshopper:
Re-Design

Energy Design Process, Oliver Lösser

Energy Design

INSTITUTE OF ARCHI-TECTURE

PRIZES

2009
Federal President Dr. Heinz Fischer bestowed the Austrian Decoration of Honor for Science and Art on Wolf D. Prix for his outstanding creative achievements.

LG Design Contest 2009 for Austria: Daniel Reist, Studio Hadid

Detail Preis 2009 – Innovation Stahl Munich, Germany, Project: BMW Welt: Wolf D. Prix

Wallpaper Design Preis 2009: Best New Public Building, London, UK, Project: BMW Welt: Wolf D. Prix

Best of 2009 Award, Los Angeles, Kalifornien, USA 2009 Project: Central Los Angeles Area High School #9 for the visual and performing arts: Wolf D. Prix

Praemium Imperiale, The Japanese Art Association: Zaha Hadid

Innovation & Design Awards, Zaragoza Bridge Pavillon: Zaha Hadid

2008
RIBA Stirling Prize Nomination, (Nordpark Cable Railway): Zaha Hadid

RIBA European Award 2008: Wolf D. Prix

RIBA International Award 2008: Wolf D. Prix

Jencks Award: Visions Built prize for his major contribution to the theory and practice of architecture: Wolf D. Prix

The Chicago Athenaeum, The International Architecture Award: Zaha Hadid

Dedale Minosse International Prize (BMW Central Building, Germany): Greg Lynn

Golden Lion for Best Installation Project (Biennale Venedig): Greg Lynn

2007
Thomas Jefferson Foundation Medal in Architecture, US: Zaha Hadid

International Architecture Award 2007, The Chicago Athenaeum, Illinois, USA: Wolf D. Prix

2006
Architecture and Technology Award Klaus Bollinger and Niels Jonkhans

Finalist for the RIBA Stirling Prize (Phaeno Science Center): Zaha Hadid

Fellowship Medal of the American Institute of Architects AIA: Wolf D. Prix

Otto-Prutscher-Prize: Gregor Holzinger

Film Prize Silverlake film festival for Giant Robot Videos (DVD): Studio Lynn

2005
Finalist for the RIBA Stirling Prize (BMW Central Building): Zaha Hadid

30 Under 30: The Watch List of Future Landmarks, The Municipal Art Society of New York: Greg Lynn

ACON Competition Winner of the Angewandte:
Lukas Galehr with Rupert Zallmann

Österreichischer Bau-Prize spezial price for the project "sharkskin": Sebastian Gallnbrunner, Mario Gasser and Peter Schamberger

2004
Laureate of the Pritzker Architecture Prize: Zaha Hadid

Progressive Architecture Citation: Greg Lynn

Annie Spink Award for Excellence in Architectural Education (RIBA/London): Wolf D. Prix

PUBLICATIONS

2009
Architecture Live 6/ Alumni – Networks Revisited, on the occasion of the Architecture Live Event

Prinz Eisenbeton Live, Edition 21 and 22 – News from the Institute of Architecture

99+ IOA Studios Hadid Lynn Prix, Selected Student Works 2004–8 Design = Thinking

Institute of Architecture folder 09

2008
Prinz Eisenbeton, Edition 19 and 20 – News from the Institute of Architecture

Architecture Live 5 – Topping Vienna, on the occasion of the Architecture Live Event

2007
Prinz Eisenbeton, Edition 15, 16, 17 and 18 – News from the Institute of Architecture

Architecture Live 4, on the occasion of the Architecture Live Event

Institute of Architecture brochure

Catalogue of Postcards (student projects 2004–07) on the occasion of an exhibition of Studio Hadid at Schusev State Museum of Architecture in Moscow

Institute of Architecture folder 07/08

2006
Prinz Eisenbeton, Edition 9, 10, 11, 12, 13 and 14 – News from the Institute of Architecture

Architecture Live 3, on the occasion of the Architecture Live Event

Rock over Barock – Young and Beautiful: 7+2, on the occasion of the Venice Biennale

Institute of Architecture folder 07/08

2005
Prinz Eisenbeton 5 "techo en mexico" on the occasion of the exhibition at the AzW Vienna

Prinz Eisenbeton Live, Edition 2, 3, 4, 5, 6, 7 and 8 – News from the Institute of Architecture

Architecture Live 2, on the occasion of the Architecture Live Event

Rock over Barock – Young and Beautiful: 7+2, on the occasion of the Aedes East Berlin exhibition

Architektur und Bauforum "OFRUM" April 2005

2004
Prinz Eisenbeton, Edition 0 and 1 – News from Studio Prix

Architecture Live 1, on the occasion of the Architecture Live Event

EXHIBITIONS

2009

International Architectural Education Summit, University of Tokyo, July 17 – 19, 2009

Sliver Gallery: Greg Lynn: Recycled Toy Furniture Prototypes; awarded the Golden Lion for the best Installation project in the international exhibition at the Venice Architecture Biennale

Sliver Gallery: (N)Certainties 03, Cross-Over Studio François Roche, March 17 – April 22, 2009

The Essence 09 – Vordere Zollamtsstraße Vienna

Studio Prix is presenting work of students at the Dessa Gallery in Lijubliana. January 29 – February 26, 2009

Architecture Live VI / Alumni – Networks revisited, May15, 2009, University of Applied Arts Vienna

2008

The Essence 08 – MAK Vienna

Sliver Gallery: 50mm

Sliver Gallery: Simultaneity & Latency: The work of Studio Hadid

Sliver Gallery: Speciation: Hernan Alonso-Diaz Cross-Over Studio Spring

2007

Studio Hadid presents student projects 2004–7 at Schusev State Museum of Architecture in Moscow

The Essence 07 – MAK Vienna

Sliver Gallery: VIE:BRA: Vienna-Bratislava, The work of the Urban Strategies Program Spring

Sliver Gallery: Fake Space

Sliver Gallery: Technicolor Bloom Fall

2006

The Essence 06 – MAK Vienna

Sculptural Architecture in Austria, China

Rock over Barock – Venice Biennale, Italy

2005

The Essence 05 – MAK Vienna

Techo en mexico – the mexican roof 96°13' W 16°33' N at the AzW, Vienna

Rock over Barock 2, Aedes, Berlin, Germany

Spot on Schools – IMAGE, Florenz, Italy

2004

Mobility Forum, Stuttgart, Germany

EVENTS

2009

International conference: Sustainability vs Aesthetics? The Mexican Roof Revisited, Centro de las Artes de San Agustin, Oaxaca, Mexico. With Raimund Abraham, Roxana Montiel, Wolf D. Prix, Carl Pruscha, Mauricio Rocha, Michael Rotondi, Tercer Pisos, October 30 – 31, 2009

Architecture Live 6 / Alumni – Networks revisited, May 14 – 15, 2009; participants: Herwig Baumgartner, Erich Bernard, Marie-Therese Harnoncourt, Hubert Hermann, Barbara Imhof, Caren Ohrhallinger, Christian Politsch, Max Rieder, Wolfgang Tschapeller, Thomas Vietzke, Michael Wallraff, Susanne Zottl

Lecture Volker Schlemminger / OSTSEESTAAL, May 13, Studio Prix

International Architectural Education Summit, University of Tokyo, July 17 – 19, 2009, Keynote Speaker: Wolf D. Prix

IOA Sliver Lectures
David Clovers, March 17
Jan/Tim Edler "Realities:United", May 7
Hitoshi Abe, May 26
Richard Sweeney, May 28
Petra Blaisse "Shifting Position", June 4
Mark Lee "Too Dumb for New York, Too Ugly for LA",November 24
Florencia Pita, "...oh so pretty", November 26
Brent Sherwood "Orbital Cities", December 3

2008

ITNOA (In The Name of Architecture): exhibition with panel discussion, Albertina-Passage Vienna, cooperational project of students from the Technical University, University of Applied Arts and the Academy of Fine Arts in Vienna

Architecture Live 5 – Topping Vienna: Workshop with twenty architectural offices, paneldiscussion, exhibition, party; participants: Artec Architekten, Caramel, Delugan Meissl Associated Architects, Christian Fröhlich, Froetscher Lichtenwanger, Heri & Salli, Hofrichter-Ritter, Innocad, Love, Liquifer, N/A, Erich Prödl & Nils Peters, Propeller Z, Querkraft, Andreas Rumpfhuber, Span, Klaus Stattmann, Vallo Sadovsky Architects, Imro Vasko, Wendy & Jim

2007

New Crowned Hope – Welcome to Vienna – Dachgarten Integrationshaus Künstlerhaus Vienna exhibition, paneldiscussion with Peter Sellars with Gregor Holzinger, Willi Resetarits, Andrea Eraslan-Weninger, Gerald Bast and Wolf D. Prix

Architecture Live 4 – Stadt = Form Raum Netz, Urban Prototyping Conference, MAK Vienna; participants: Lacaton & Vassal Architectes, BIG-Bjarke Ingels Group, EM2N, Urban Think Tank, Hitoshi Abe, Minsuk Cho-Mass Studies, Alexander D'Hooghe, Francois Roche/R&Sie(n), Mark Wigley

2006

Secret Passion – Edek Bartz speaks with Wolf D. Prix about "Gimme Shelter" from the Rolling Stones, University of Applied Arts

Architecture Live 3 – 47 statements about architectural training, exhibition, party

2005

How to Become a Star – AzW Vienna, paneldiscussion with Jeff Kipnis, R.Somol, Michael Speaks, Roemer van Thoorn and Wolf Prix, Moderation: Reiner Zettl

Architecture Live 2 – 42 statements about architectural training, exhibition, party

2004

Architecture Live 1 – 41 statements about architectural training, party

RESEARCH

RESEARCH NETWORK: AMM
Advanced Materials and Manufacturing Network

The focus is the connection of state-of-the-art technology in the fields of material science, manufacturing technologies and digital design and engineering processes, always with a strong focus on the artistic relevance for architectural and industrial design. The research environment is designed for a transdisciplinary, synergy friendly working culture.

Coordinators: Oliver Bertram
Members: Mathias Del Campo, Sandra Manninger, various members of the Institute of Architecture, University of Applied Arts Vienna

Participating Universities: TU Innsbruck (AT), TU Kassel (DE), ETH Zürich (CH)

IP-CITY PROJECT
The research aim of the IP-City Project is to investigate analytical and technological approaches to presence in real life settings. By overlaying features of real settings with virtual objects so called mixed environments are created that have a new quality of information and a specific logic of what might be called incorporated information. The postgraduate program "Urban Strategies" investigates the versatility of Mixed Reality Applications for urban design and planning purposes.

Coordinator: Reiner Zettl
Researcher: Andrea Börner

Project Partners AND Participating Universities: Aalborg University, Fraunhofer Institut für Angewandte Informationstechnik FIT, Graz University of Technology, Helsinki University of Technology, Imagination Computer Services GesmbH, University of Applied Arts Vienna, University of Cambridge, Université Marne la Vallée – Champs sur Marne, University of Oulu, Vienna University of Technology

BRAIN CITY LAB
The research project is conducted in collaboration with the neuroscientist Wolf Singer and under scientific advise of the Max-Planck Institute of Brain Research in Frankfurt.

The working principles of the brain that enables it to successfully recognise, store and predict patterns (i.e. to think) will be the point of departure for an investigation on how these principles can be transferred to the field of urban planning.

Team: Niels Jonkhans, Reinhard Hacker, Armin Hess, Reiner Zettl

CONTACT DETAILS

Institute of Architecture
University of Applied Arts Vienna
Oskar Kokoschka-Platz 2
1010 Vienna, Austria

T +43 (0)1 711 33-2331
F +43 (0)1 711 33-2339

www.i-o-a.at
www.aaac.at

General enquiries:
architecture@uni-ak.ac.at
www.i-o-a.at

Studios:
studio.hadid@uni-ak.ac.at
studio.lynn@uni-ak.ac.at
studio.prix@uni-ak.ac.at

IOA STUDIOS
HADID LYNN PRIX
SELECTED STUDENT WORKS
2009

EDITOR
Wolf D. Prix

EDITORS IN CHIEF
Anja Jonkhans, Roswitha Janowski-Fritsch

TRANSLATION AND PROOF-READING
Camilla Nielsen

PHOTOGRAPHY
Reiner Zettl

DESIGN
Paulus M. Dreibholz

PRINTING AND BINDING
Holzhausen Druck GmbH, Vienna

Printed on acid-free and chlorine-free bleached paper

© 2011 Springer-Verlag/Wien
Printed in Austria
SpringerWienNewYork is a part of
Springer Science + Business Media
springer.at

SPIN: 12594771

Library of Congress Control Number: 2009929402

ISSN 1866-248X
ISBN 978-3-211-99199-2
SpringerWienNewYork

WITH THE SUPPORT OF

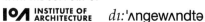